Jeff Connor was born in Manchester and now lives in Edinburgh. As the award-winning author of eleven other books, he has enjoyed a marginally more successful career than East Stirlingshire FC.

Praise for *Pointless*:

'Bracing [and] comic . . . The supporting cast is direct from the latest Mike Leigh film' *The Times*

'An intriguing story . . . As the publisher's blurb says (for once accurately), it's "funny, sad and heartwarming"' *Daily Telegraph*

'An entertaining fly-on-the-wall book . . . On every page the characters come to life' *Glasgow Evening Times*

'Connor writes with clarity and humour' *Sunday Times Scotland*

'Wryly humorous' *Scotsman*

'This could be a grim tale, but Connor has a keen eye for the ridiculous and his prose coolly brings out the absurdity of the sometimes hilarious situations he witnesses without ever patronising his subject.' *Independent on Sunday*

'This is journalist Jeff Connor's sympathetic but still painfully amusing account of another calamitous year in East Stirling's long and inglorious history . . .' *Daily Mail*

Pointless

**A season with Britain's
worst football team**

JEFF CONNOR

headline

First published in 2005
by HEADLINE BOOK PUBLISHING

First published in paperback in 2006
by HEADLINE BOOK PUBLISHING

3

ISBN 978 0 7553 1353 2

All photographs © David Gibson/Fotosport except:
Plate section 1, page 8 (bottom); plate section 2, page 7 (bottom); plate section 2,
page 8 © Darren Russell/*Loaded*/IPC Syndication
Plate section 2, page 5 (top and bottom) © *Falkirk Herald*

Typeset in Stone Serif by Palimpsest Book Production Limited, Polmont, Stirlingshire

Printed and bound in Great Britain by Mackays of Chatham, Chatham, Kent

Headline's policy is to use papers that are natural, renewable and recyclable products
and made from wood grown in sustainable forests. The logging and manufacturing
processes are expected to conform to the environmental regulations of the country of
origin.

HEADLINE BOOK PUBLISHING
A division of Hodder Headline
338 Euston Road
London NW1 3BH

www.headline.co.uk
www.hodderheadline.com

To the management, players
and supporters of East Stirlingshire FC.
Hemingway must have had you in mind when he wrote:
'Man can be beaten but never destroyed.'

Contents

≡

'I have to say that I don't think there is any great point in East Stirling.'

— Former manager Danny Diver
speaking in February 2003,
one month before resigning.

ACKNOWLEDGEMENTS

First of all, heartfelt thanks to all at East Stirlingshire Football Club, in particular, the chairman Alan J. Mackin, chief executive Les Thomson and all the board. The manager Dennis Newall, along with his assistant Greig Denham, allowed me whole-hearted access to their corner of the club operation, in often fraught circumstances, and I am proud to say that by the end of the season I regarded them both as friends. That applies, too, to Jimmy Wilson, Bobby Jack and all the players. The extraordinary Shire fans, led by the chairman of the supporters' club, Ian Ramsay, proved a breed apart and unreasonably accommodating to an outsider. It has been a long, but rewarding, journey and I couldn't have had better travelling companions.

I am grateful to David Wilson and Bob McDevitt at Headline for their faith in what must have seemed an unlikely project. David was also an astute and dedicated editor and thanks go, too, to David Gibson of Fotosport for his photographs.

Finally, as ever, my agent Mark Stanton of Jenny Brown Associates had to put up with most of the angst and prevarication associated with all of my projects and still came out the other end smiling. He deserves my eternal gratitude.

WARNING

This book contains nudity, bad language and scenes of a sexual nature. It also contains awful goalkeeping, dreadful defending and poor finishing. Readers of a delicate disposition – and Alan Hansen – should look elsewhere.

FERGIE WAS HERE

The directions were idiot-proof. I was to leave the car in Falkirk's Central Retail Park and take the first turn past Carpet Right, in between the rival electrical superstores, Currys and Comet. The ground was opposite Land of Leather. If I reached Homebase, I had gone too far.

Twenty minutes later I still hadn't found the way in. A row of floodlights, the traditional beacons in the sky for seekers of football arenas from afar, were there all right, peeping coyly over a large concrete wall. What looked like the top of a domed stand rose frustratingly out of reach on the far side of the Comet staff car park. But no front entrance.

The *Bell's Scottish Football League Review*, the 2001/2 version, wasn't much help: 'East Stirlingshire FC, nicknamed the Shire,' it read. 'Falkirk, FK2 7AY'. The chairman, board of directors and the Football Safety Officers' Association representative were all listed, along with the shirt sponsor (Finewood Joinery Products Ltd), the e-mail address (lest@theshire.madasafish.com), most capped player (Humphrey Jones, five times for Wales), most goals scored (thirty-six by Malcolm Morrison in the season 1938/9) and the record attendance (11,500 for a match against Hibernian on 2 February 1969 – had they all climbed over the wall?). But no address.

After another ten minutes of frantic searching I finally

made out, at the foot of the page devoted to the club, some minute lettering alongside a map shaded green and in the shape of a football ground. The main entrance and vehicle access to East Stirlingshire FC, it revealed, was in Firs Street, just off Thornhill Road. I took the car, reasoning that I would be able to leave it in the directors' car park. It was early July and a time of year when most football club directors would be elsewhere, possibly in Amsterdam, maybe Bangkok.

Thornhill Road and Firs Street were embedded in a maze of ancient terraced houses and newish-build council flats, and at the end of the latter I spotted a large sign above two turnstiles which read: 'Welcome to Firs Park'. And below, in slightly smaller black and white lettering: 'East Stirlingshire FC'. A tattered cardboard sign warned that 'No Alcohol' was allowed, and a blob of white paint announced entrance fees of £8. The gates were locked. I was beginning to feel like Lara Croft, desperately seeking the Playstation button that would open the tomb.

I persevered, parked between two battered white vans in Firs Street and walked back along Thornhill Road, past a drive-in McDonald's and on to Land of Leather and the wall. Still nothing. I was on the point of phoning the Falkirk branch of the Citizens' Advice Bureau, or asking a passing policeman, when I chanced upon it.

At the corner of the wall, where it met the Comet car park, an aluminium door – not unlike the entrance to a self-assemble fall-out shelter – decorated with painted graffiti telling the people of Falkirk that 'Haley does it standing up' was caught suddenly by a rogue breeze and, unhindered by a large padlock, swung slightly ajar. I pushed it further open and walked inside. Beyond was Firs Park in all its glory. I breathed it all in, coughed, and began to wonder, for the first of many times, what I had let myself in for.

Falkirk, a town in Scotland's central belt with a population of around 150,000, doesn't have a lot going for it. The centre is untidily laid out and an annoying one-way system makes for traffic congestion. There is little to attract a visitor, although it has twice been named 'Best Town in Scotland for Shopping' and boasts connections with William Wallace and Mary, Queen of Scots; but then so do a lot of towns in Scotland.

The first Battle of Falkirk was fought nearby in 1298 and over the ensuing years Friday and Saturday nights have seen several more. Parts of the town, in particular the area close by Firs Park, are notable only for their crime and unemployment figures. Falkirk does have its eponymous Wheel, but the 'world's first and only rotating boat lift' is some way out of town so visitors travelling by car need never enter the town itself. Situated almost equidistant between the larger, and more glamorous, cities of Stirling, Glasgow and Edinburgh, most tourists give Falkirk a wide berth.

But the town does have two football teams. I had passed a large stadium on my way in from the M9, standing in rather splendid isolation on the outskirts where the built-up areas began. It was surrounded by signs directing 'football traffic this way'. This, I assumed, was the home of Falkirk FC. Falkirk had once been East Stirlingshire's fiercest rivals; now that rivalry existed only in the minds of a few Shire fans.

Favourites to win promotion from Division One to the Scottish Premier League, Falkirk FC had left their neighbours behind in every sense of the word. The frontage of Westfield Stadium was all glass and pristine brick, the car park the size of Sydney Cricket Ground. At Firs Park, there was no frontage whatsoever. The players' and directors' entrance was, literally, a hole in a wall. What was I doing here?

Over thirty years previously another visitor from afar had

stood in the same spot and undoubtedly asked himself the same question. Alexander Chapman Ferguson was thirty-four and a recently retired footballer. A striker of moderate talent, he had, by virtue of a bad-loser ethic and famously flying elbows, forged a reasonable professional career with Queen's Park, St Johnstone, Dunfermline, Rangers, Falkirk and Ayr United.

At Falkirk he had won undying fame when the side of 1972 reached the Scottish Cup Final, won the First Division title and reached the semi-final of the old League Cup. In the Scottish Cup, he had scored the equaliser against Rangers to earn immortality in these parts. But Ferguson was a serviceable rather than spectacular player, and an example of the Glasgow football pundit Bob Crampsey's favourite theory that the best managers are not necessarily the best players.

As Crampsey is fond of pointing out, three of Scotland's greatest, Matt Busby, Jock Stein and Bill Shankly, had seven Scottish caps between them – and Shankly won six of those. Stein, revered in Scotland as the mastermind of the 1967 Lisbon Lions, was never capped. Ferguson, too, had never been selected to play for his country; but he did attract the requisite contempt of directors and football boards – a trait developed during his time as a shop steward in the Govan shipyards – a couple of coaching badges, and formidable ambition. Contemporaries during the latter part of his playing days at Falkirk had no hesitation in insisting that 'if any player would make it in management, it would be Alex Ferguson'.

The job he had taken on was forbidding. East Stirlingshire had just finished bottom in the Scottish League, and the board had freed all but eight players, leaving Ferguson without a goalkeeper (a situation that Manchester United fans of today could justifiably claim hasn't changed). At Firs

Park, he had been bequeathed the likes of 'Stuckie', 'The Flyer', 'Simmy' and 'Big Seldom' – so named because he hardly ever played. But you have to start somewhere, as they say.

'Stand up, be counted, demonstrate your desire' were Ferguson's tenets, allied to what, in man-management terms, was to become a familiar *modus operandi*. 'He terrified us,' said Bobby McCulley, a striker at the time. 'I'd never been afraid of anyone before but he was such a frightening bastard from the start. Everything was focused towards his goals. Time didn't matter to him; he never wore a watch. If he wanted something done, he'd stay as late as it took or come in early. He always joined in with us in training and would have us playing in the dark until his five-a-side team won. He was ferocious, elbowing and kicking.'

He scared the Shire directors, too. Willie Muirhead, the then chairman, had contacted Ferguson on the recommendation of Ally MacLeod, his manager at Ayr United. MacLeod had mentioned that he had a thirty-something player in his reserves desperate to get into coaching. He had the necessary qualifications, and at interview had come across as confident, sincere and knowledgeable.

More importantly – and this has always been the key qualification for the succession of Shire boards when interviewing prospective managers – he would do it for virtually nothing. In the end, the directors and the new boy settled on £40 a week; a pittance in any terms . . . but £40 more than the current manager.

Ferguson made his mark from the start. League restructuring at the time had created three divisions for the following season: Premier, First and Second. This meant that a place in the top six in the 1974/5 season would earn the Shire promotion to the First. The new manager oozed confidence: 'I am a bad loser,' he told the board and fans. 'I will give you a winning side.'

He won the support over immediately by engineering an early win over their hated local rivals, Falkirk, and after two months the club were lying fourth in Division Two. Muirhead and his board could justifiably claim that, for once, they had appointed the right man. Before long, however, the chairman began to wonder what manner of beast he had created. Muirhead thought of himself as Professor Higgins; in reality he was Doctor Frankenstein. Within days, Ferguson had spent his £2,000 playing budget on one player and constructed the rest of his squad with free transfers and youngsters who possessed more energy than skill.

As is so often the case, particularly at Firs Park, the new manager's ambitions soon outreached the board's willingness to dip into their pockets. When he transported a group of schoolboys from Glasgow to Falkirk for trials the directors, outraged that they had not been consulted, refused to meet the expense. Ferguson pulled the money – his week's wages – from his pocket, hurled it on to the boardroom table and threatened to resign.

Muirhead dissuaded him, but it was clear that this was a man who believed he was destined for better things. And when the head-hunters from First Division St Mirren contacted him, a hundred and seventeen days after his arrival at Firs Park, a famous managerial career began in earnest. One of the players Fergie left behind was later to say, with masterly understatement: 'I don't think he'd have got where he is today if he'd stayed with the Shire.'

As for the club, it could be argued that they have never recovered. Pip had gone his glorious way and the jilted Miss Havishams of Scottish football were left behind to wallow in their decay and private misery. All the clocks are stopped, at around 2.55 p.m., in Shire House.

The club's colourful, often clouded, past mirrors its present. In the beginning, there was a cricket team called Bainsford Bluebonnets (which set the pattern in giving chroniclers the opportunity to write about large scores against), but the founders turned to football in the autumn of 1880, changed the name to Bainsford Britannia, and played their first official game, against Falkirk Seconds, in December that year. They lost 7-0. According to the local paper at the time, Britannia 'played pluckily but were up against better quality players', a description that could be usefully employed 125 years later to sum up the state of the team today. The name was changed to East Stirlingshire in 1881, Falkirk having beaten them to the punch and nabbed the name of the home town for themselves.

The rest of the club's playing history can be covered very quickly. They joined the Scottish Football Association (SFA) in 1883 and in 1888 reached the quarter-finals of the Scottish Cup where they lost to Celtic. In 1931/2 the club won the Division Two Championship and in 1980 were promoted to Division One as runners-up to Falkirk. In terms of points, the fifty-nine gained in the 1995 season remain the highest ever.

It is off the field, however, where the Shire have consistently caught the headlines, usually for all the wrong reasons. Post-Fergie, some of their managerial appointments were catastrophic. His successor, recommended by Ferguson himself, was the former Dundee, Arsenal and Manchester United defender Ian Ure, who failed to show at the club's AGM a few weeks after being promoted, was caught up in a subsequent row over bonus payments and was sacked twelve months later. Ure signed off by calling the Shire board 'a joke' and 'a bunch of amateurs lacking foresight and ambition'. Muirhead gave as good as he got, describing Ure's tenure as 'a disaster'.

Martin Ferguson, brother of Alex, fared little better and in more recent times the manager's office has had what amounts to a revolving door, with the Shire averaging one such official a year up to the present day. Some walked, others were escorted out through the aluminium portal. Various boards through the ages have only added to the general air of hopelessness and incompetence, the sense that the club were going nowhere.

The Shire, being tiny even in Scottish football terms and invariably rendered defenceless by impoverishment, have often been a target for speculators. In 1957, two Glasgow businessmen, Jack and Charles Steedman, bought fifty-one per cent of the company's shares for a total of £1,000. The club was run as a business, with the brothers discovering players in the juvenile and junior ranks, schooling them at the Shire, and then moving them on at a profit (until 1966 no manager was appointed and the directors picked and ran the team). In one season they sold Eddie McCreadie, Tommy Knox and Jimmy Mulholland, all to Chelsea, for a combined sum of £20,000.

As the Steedmans had promised, the Shire reached Division One, but they then discovered, as had so many before them, that their ambitions could not match their capabilities and the wheels began to fall off. There was a dispute over payments and a number of players walked out. By 1964, the Shire were back in Division Two, having won just 5 games out of 34 and accumulated a points total of 12, with 37 goals for and 97 against.

Gates dwindled, too, and in an effort to stop the rot the Steedmans decided to up sticks and take the club twenty-five miles west, to Clydebank, where they believed the larger catchment area and thriving junior set-up would restore their fortunes. A club called East Stirlingshire, however, would probably not sit easily in the middle of Glasgow, so they simply renamed it ES Clydebank.

Most football fans, after initial protest, will resign themselves to changes in their club's ownership, players and management but, as the new owner of Wimbledon discovered in 2003, to change the club name is to invite trouble. The Shire fans duly mobilised, the Steedmans were hauled before the Edinburgh Court of Session and, when it was discovered that the brothers had transferred a large proportion of the shares to their employees at Milngavie Motors Ltd., judgement went against them.

The Shire returned to Falkirk behind a large brass band with, so it is said, thousands of fans lining the streets of the town to welcome them home. They have remained there, and in the Scottish Football League (SFL), ever since. Far longer, in fact, than Clydebank, who bit the dust in 2002.

But the Shire have also had several close shaves. Payments, or the lack of them, have always been a bone of contention for the playing staff. Before the 1975/6 season, in the Ure era, the players went on strike over pay, and consistent cost-cutting down the years – not least when the club decided to impose the notorious £10-a-week salary cap in 2003 – has lost them a number of their best performers.

Not surprisingly, the off-field problems have been reflected on the field of play. As the current manager is fond of saying: 'if you pay peanuts, you tend to get monkeys', and some of the *faux pas* Shire fans have witnessed down the years would make a chimpanzees' tea party seem a serious, stolid affair. Some of the defeats belong in 'you couldn't make it up' territory.

In the season of 1979/80, the Shire were paired with Albion Rovers in the first round of the League Cup. The first leg was a 1-1 draw and the return leg at Coatbridge finished in a 0-0 stalemate, but the Shire kept their heads in the subsequent shoot-out and went through 9-8 on penalties. It was then discovered that the referee had somehow overlooked the regulation thirty minutes of extra time. Despite a Shire appeal to the League Management Committee, the game was replayed and the match proceeded in what was to become recognisable Shire comic-cuts style, with two own goals in the first fifteen minutes and a comfortable 4-1 win for the opposition.

The board received travelling expenses and a win bonus for the match that didn't count. Their application for compensation, based on the money they would have received for a hypothetical second-round tie with Partick Thistle, was rejected.

In another match, again against Albion Rovers – a club which seems to bring out the worst in the Shire – the manager used four different goalkeepers: the starting keeper had been sent off, closely followed by his deputy; the third, an outfield player, was injured in a collision and the fourth, in a startling reversal of fortune's norm, then saved a penalty.

Facing Stirling Albion in January 2004, the Shire actually led 2-1 with twenty minutes to go and a famous victory was in sight. But then they had two men sent off and conceded three goals (one an own goal) in the last ten minutes to lose 4-2. Throughout history, it could be said that the bounce of the ball has never favoured East Stirlingshire FC. But at least, as I was to hear often over the coming months, 'Fergie Was Here'.

As I wandered round the ground it was clear that not much could have changed since the days (117 of them) when Sir Alex bestrode Firs Park. At right angles to the wall, a dilapidated corrugated stand fronted a collection of the terraced council houses and flats on what I now recognised as Firs Street. This stand served as the background for a straggling line of faded, redundant advertising hoardings, most of them indecipherable. ROSEBA-K OF-I-G read one, CLO-A-L B-R, another, like a collection of Carol Vorderman's favourite anagrams.

At the opposite end to the wall a weed-infested terrace sloped upwards in a series of shallow steps close by the two turnstiles. The main stand was covered and appeared relatively new, but much of it was taken up by enclosures marked 'home directors' and 'visiting directors'. A glass box the size of a telephone booth was probably home to the local radio station, but its view was half-obstructed by a large piece of paper taped on to the window: 'Fuck the board', it read.

The grass of the pitch, in fierce competition for light and water with the profusion of dandelions and other weeds, was around five inches long and from the centre circle, watched by three fat seagulls and a middle-aged man in a red shirt, an asthmatic garden sprinkler spurted a jet of water upwards and sideways over two square yards every five seconds. The man in the red shirt didn't look round as I made my way down the steps and past a wooden garden shed from which spilled a selection of redundant tools and five no-parking cones.

A few yards from the shed, someone had planted a Portakabin. Like a jeweller's shop in Tower Hamlets or, indeed, an off-license in Glasgow, the Portakabin windows had been reinforced heavily with mesh and bolts. The sign outside revealed this to be the boardroom.

I was there to see the club's chief executive, Les Thomson, with an offer this unfortunate institution surely could not refuse. I would pay them £2,000, the size of Sir Alex Ferguson's first budget, and in return would be allowed unrestricted access to all areas. I would be privy to team talks, the workings of the manager's office and board meetings, and I would be allowed on the bus with the team as they travelled round the Scottish Third Division.

I would be the Shire's fly on the wall and, eventually, in the words of my brief, produce 'a humorous and insightful account of the 2004/5 season and detail all aspects of the running of the club and on-field performances'. A newspaper colleague had advised me to 'pay them fuck all, they need all the publicity they can get', but the two grand was a deliberate and calculated bribe. I had read the thoughts of Hunter Davies when he came to write *The Glory Game*, the up-market forerunner to this book.

Davies had wanted to spend a year with Tottenham Hotspur, then in their seventies pomp, but his season was haunted by the mordant fear that the team and/or the directors and management, would have second thoughts midway through and show him the door. He was to write later: 'I knew I could be kicked out at any time. I would position myself towards the corner of the dressing room, hoping that when, in the event of a bad performance, the manager Bill Nicholson starting chucking teacups, his eyes wouldn't rest on me and wonder what I was doing there. I knew that if I didn't make it through the whole season the book would be ruined. By the end I had successfully made myself resemble a piece of furniture.'

I came to the conclusion that it would be easier for everyone at Firs Park to regard me as a piece of furniture if there was a cast-iron contract between myself and East Stirlingshire Football Club plc. If they did decide that my face didn't fit at some stage of the season, and escorted me back out through the aluminium door, I could sue them for every penny – or at least for every few pence – they had.

I also reasoned that being in the Scottish Third Division, the Cannery Row of British senior football, they couldn't possibly reject this unexpected windfall and was well aware that the club accounts revealed a loss for the year ending May 2004 of over £26,000.

As the clincher, I would volunteer to help out with some of the more menial tasks required at any football club. The Shire already had two kit managers, one paid, the other not, but I planned to offer my services as unpaid deputy assistant. I would hump team kit from bus to dressing room and back again when playing away. How could they refuse such a generous offer? Quite easily, as it turned out. Generosity is in the eye of the receiver. It was not enough. In the words of one director: 'Here, we dinnae like the idea of Greeks bearing gifts.'

In an office the size of a broom cupboard, just inside the main door and opposite the boardroom, I found Les Thomson surrounded by filing cabinets, piles of jerseys wrapped in cellophane bags and a dormant fax machine. A genial, affluent-looking man in his early sixties and bedecked in gold jewellery, he was agreeable enough, but having said yes in principle he did add a codicil: I would have to come to the next board meeting and present my case. They would then, in the language of bodies like these, 'deliberate and duly come back with their decision within a few days'. As the next board meeting was a week away, it would give me ample time to put together a presentation that would win the hearts and minds of the most hard-hearted director.

Thomson, a former Falkirk captain, had joined the club in 1993 and at various times had been chairman (twice) and chief executive. He had now taken on the dual role of

CEO/club secretary and ran the club on a day-to-day basis with guidance from afar from his chairman. Thomson counted the gate receipts, organised transport and paid the staff.

He was encouraging, but cautionary: 'There shouldn't be a problem, but you'll have to get past the chairman and there's one awkward old wee bastard on the board who won't go for it. He votes against everything. He's been doing it all his life. Last season I even caught him in the directors' box celebrating an opposition goal.' There was silence for a moment while I took in the implications of this appalling heresy, then Thomson added: 'But he is seventy-five years old, you know.'

We made some small talk about football, or rather the football he had played. His career, he said, had left him with two dodgy knees and one everlasting claim to fame: 'I played against Fergie – did you know he was manager here? I played with him and against him and regularly kicked him up in the air in training. He's a good mate of mine. When I go down to Old Trafford he always invites me in for a dram and a blather.'

I tried to look impressed, but even I knew that if you counted the number of Scottish former footballers in their early sixties who claimed to have 'done' Sir Alex – and stayed mates with him – it would probably equate to the million or so Scots who swear they were at Hampden Park to see Real Madrid beat Eintracht Frankfurt 7-3 (capacity 134,000 and the match wasn't a sell-out). Scotland is bursting at the seams with former players who have kicked Fergie up in the air. He would need an office the size of a ballroom and a large distillery to entertain all the former team-mates who have booted the royal backside in training.

I asked Thomson about playing staff for the coming season.

'Well, we've made some changes and I recently signed a foreign player. He's a Norwegian and he'll be the only Norwegian playing in Scottish senior football.'

'Have you had any foreigners playing here before?'

'Aye, frae Glasgow and Edinburgh.'

I laughed long and loud at this one. Thomson looked serious. My laughter died.

'Do you think there will be any problems with the manager?' I asked.

'Which manager?'

'Your manager, the Shire manager. He might not like the idea of having an outsider in the dressing room. Maybe it would be best if I met him.'

'You already have.'

'Eh?'

'I'm the manager. He's the coach. I look after the day-to-day running of the club, I control this organisation. He looks after the team. Believe me, there will be no problems about you being in the dressing room. He does as we tell him. All you have to do is convince the board. Where are you parked by the way?'

'In Firs Street.'

'Well, you had better get back there quick, son. If you're lucky, you'll still have four wheels.'

I hastened out, past the boardroom, up the steps, through the hole in the wall, along Thornhill Road and back to Firs Street. The car was still there, and so were its wheels. But a rake-thin teenager, his white, almost translucent arms poking out of a T-shirt emblazoned with RETOX IN PROGRESS, was fiddling with the catch on the boot. 'Nice motor, pal,' he said, moving away with studied nonchalance.

A week later, on a Tuesday evening, I was back at the ground; this time I'd left the motor in the Land of Leather car park. The same man in the same red shirt was watching the same garden sprinkler, although by now it had made some progress and was wheezing water jets from midway between the centre circle and the eighteen-yard line. The seagulls had flown.

I introduced myself to the man in the red shirt. Jimmy Wilson had been with the club for around twenty-three years in various capacities. Right now, in the manner of many club employees in the lower leagues, he was multitasking as groundsman/head kit manager, although he also worked as laundryman and a sort of catering manager – he made soup and toast for the players after training and brewed up for himself and Les Thomson.

And he had done virtually everything else. A squad photograph taken before a Scottish Cup tie against Hibs in 1968 included a crouching, track-suited figure in the front row captioned 'J. Wilson, trainer'. He had run the now defunct social club and, for a time, along with a local journalist, had been team manager. 'We were unbeaten in two games,' he told me. 'Not a lot of folk at the Shire can say that.'

A small, compact figure in his early sixties, his face weathered nut-brown by the elements, Jimmy was quick of wit and ready of smile, and it soon became clear that these qualities were a prerequisite for his various jobs. His tractor mower hadn't made it to pre-season training (which, he pointed out, accounted for the overlong grass) and his budget for the coming year was around £200.

Jimmy was helped by his equally sharp-witted friend, Bobby Jack, a retired BP refinery worker. He mucked in with the ground maintenance during the week and took on the role of assistant kit manager on match days. Silver-haired and garrulous, he was originally from Edinburgh and supported Hearts when he wasn't supporting the Shire.

When I met Bobby he was wearing shorts and a T-shirt that read 'Talent Scout', and he lost no time in telling me that he had once been chairman.

'That gives me bragging rights over Jimmy. He was only the manager.'

'So both of you do the lot here?'

'We get other help a couple of days a week,' said Jimmy. 'Daft Dougie comes in and helps us.'

The deputy assistant Firs Park groundsman at the time was a twenty-one-year-old Glaswegian who each evening after work returned to the nearby Polmont Institute for Young Offenders to continue, so it was said, a six-year sentence for dealing in drugs.

On his first day, according to Jimmy, through an open window Daft Dougie's practised eye had caught someone shooting up in one of the flats opposite the ground. My car boot-raider, I wondered?

Daft Dougie, as part of his rehabilitation, or more accurately as part of his punishment, had to trim the 4,800 square yards of Firs Park using an old-fashioned garden mower and stamp down the pitch's numerous divots; Jimmy had had to show him how to use a garden hoe for the weeding. He had never had a job in his life. I decided I didn't want to know how he'd supplemented his dole cheques.

By Daft Dougie's own account, life at Polmont wasn't too bad. The inmates had Sky TV, the food was good and their lot was improved immeasurably when Falkirk District Council built a mixed-sex high school right opposite. Dougie also had a steady girlfriend and was allowed conjugal rights at weekends.

'Oi, you, over here.' The voice came from the direction of the Portakabin labelled Boardroom and belonged to a large, imposing figure dressed in jeans and an open-necked shirt. He was striding towards us with the pigeon-toed, bandy-legged gait of a former footballer. Even from afar, he bore an unmistakeable air of authority, menace even. 'I'm Alan Mackin,' he said. 'I'm the chairman of East Stirlingshire. Come in and meet the directors. You'll have a laugh.'

Mackin seemed friendly enough on the surface yet, at the same time, unnerving. We had barely got past the introductions when he announced: 'I like you, Jeff, I think you are a nice guy. We're going to get on fine.' For some reason, this alarmed me far more than Mackin's appearance – 6 foot 3 inches, around 14 stone, big hands, neck that came straight down from his ears – and his reputation.

I had done my homework. As a footballer he had been a noted defensive hard case, mainly with Falkirk. I knew he was originally from Paisley, a property developer and a tax exile in Spain (in west of Scotland terms the equivalent of carrying a large sign saying 'Don't Fuck With Me'). And one football writer had indeed warned me: 'Don't get on the wrong side of him.' Another told me: 'He'll let you into the club, no bother. He'll go for the money (although he will try and bump it up) and he'll look on you as a challenge. He likes challenges.'

Alan J. Mackin – the J was there to distinguish him from his son, also Alan, a well-known tennis player – had certainly faced many challenges during his fifteen-year association with East Stirlingshire FC. He had first appeared at Firs Park in the 1989/90 season when he acquired shares from the then chairman John Turnbull, had a spell as manager when he had by all accounts left a trail of flying boots and shattered dressing-room doors throughout Scotland and then disappeared completely for a time.

He reappeared in 1999 to make a determined effort to

take over the club and one year later, after a vicious struggle with the chairman and vice-chairman of the time, he gained what amounted to total control. There had been many casualties *en route*, including fellow board members, managers, coaching staff and the occasional player.

But for the past six years Mackin's major challenges had come from the club's fans, whose paranoia and dislike of any sort of Shire authority had been honed over many years of frustration and confrontation. Some of them regarded the chairman as the devil incarnate; others saw him in a worse light.

Supporters of football clubs at any level of the game do have one thing in common – a belief that they could run their club better than any board of directors. This applies as much to the likes of Manchester United as East Stirlingshire. Chairmen and owners are bottom of any football popularity league. But none, surely, had ever been as unpopular as Alan J. Mackin.

By the time I arrived, in the wake of the club's worst season ever – eight points from thirty-two games – the relationship between Mackin and the hardcore Shire support had reached an all-time low. The fans hated the chairman; the chairman despised the fans. They saw him as a dastardly asset stripper, a moustache-twirling villain bent only on self-enrichment; he regarded them as interfering rabble-rousers.

The fans' favourite refrain was that 'the chairman should dip his hand in his pocket to buy players'. The chairman's inclination was to never dip his hand in his pocket for anyone, particularly a player. The support's enduring fear, however, was that Mackin, as he had often threatened to do, would eventually sell Firs Park and vanish with the proceeds.

The warfare was brutal at times. Some fans alleged that

Mackin, during one of his famously rare appearances at Firs Park, had used binoculars to spy on them. Or maybe he was just counting them . . .

At a home game, when they had organised one of many protests against the chairman and the board, they claimed Mackin had set up a video camera in the directors' box at half-time to film them in their corrugated shed at the Firs Street side. Why he would want to do this was never made clear (a Paisley property developer would surely employ more direct methods). One theory was that, having caught them on camera, he planned to send the tape to a lip-reader and ban for life anyone captured mouthing nasty remarks about Alan J. Mackin and his board. Mackin claimed he was making a film 'for training purposes', which again hardly made sense as he seldom attended home games, let alone training nights.

Huge threads on Shire Shout, the message board for online fans, discussed 'What are we going to do about Mackin?'. Another put him top of a fantasy list of 'people I would like to punch' and one fan informed me, in all seriousness, that he scanned every newspaper report hoping to read of a murder in Paisley with a certain football club chairman named as the victim.

In March 2004 when the Shire had just lost their twenty-third league game in a row, a large band of dissenters arrived sporting Karate Kid-style headbands bearing a 'Mackin Out' logo. Supporters' club chairman Ian Ramsay explained at the time: 'It's an M with a cross through it, which either represents Mackin or the fact we are Mad!'

Despite such protests, Mackin went his own way, seemingly totally immune to the fans' views or opinions. And he could – and often did – point out that he, and another director, Alec McCabe, had loaned the impoverished company around £16,000 of their own money three years earlier when the Inland Revenue was making disturbing noises about seizing club assets over a long-standing tax bill. The club was said to be two days away from extinction.

Mackin could henceforth cast himself in the role of saviour, insisting: 'I also paid £3,000 in wages and outstanding bills. I have been putting my money where my mouth is but I can't continue to invest at that level. Selling the ground for a good price can be the only catalyst for something happening. From now until then we just need to keep a lid on expenditure.' He has never made any secret of his intention to offload the club's only asset and divide most of the proceeds among the shareholders, the majority of whom were Alan J. Mackin, his family and fellow board members.

The effective total of shares held by the board was around seventy-five per cent. If this was to be divided among the majority shareholders, it was clear that there would not be much left for investment in playing staff, a new stadium or even a tractor mower for Jimmy Wilson.

McCabe, a retired solicitor in his mid-fifties from Glasgow, had told the Scottish media as much in July 2004: 'That was the basis of our election to the board, that part of the proceeds from the sale of the ground would be returned to the shareholders. Our position has never changed on that, it's never been a secret. Selling the ground has been the aim not only of this board but the previous board and probably the board before them. The club is loss-making on a recurring basis so we have to do something. We do have plans for the club's future but we're not in position to make them public at this stage.'

Towards the end of the 2003/4 season, when the Shire were surpassing themselves in sheer ineptitude, Mackin went public to claim: 'I'm not responsible for the results. But the new manager is working hard to turn things around. The £10-a-week thing has been an excuse. There haven't been enough players coming in with the right mentality. The people who own the majority of the shares in the club are happy with the job I am doing as chairman.'

Mackin, his wife, mother, son and two daughters held 1,029 out of 2,000 shares, making them the effective owners, so they probably were quite happy with the performance of the chairman. As for the rest of the board, McCabe and his family have a stake of 360, the vice-chairman Douglas Morrison 10 and another director, John Morton, along with his wife and three daughters, 40. Morton's father-in-law, Alex Forsyth, who also sits on the board, holds 68 shares and Les Thomson, his wife, son and daughter own 41 between them. You could say it is a family club.

The rumours that Mackin was going to sell off the club's home for eighty-three years and recoup his investment had been floating around for a couple of seasons. Firs Park borders a large retail park on one side and a housing estate on the other and the attractions to a developer are obvious.

The problem for Mackin and his board was that Falkirk District Council had designated the land 'for leisure use only'. It was said, too, that the whole area – and after prolonged rain it did not require a chartered surveyor to work this out – had severe drainage problems that would require a totally new system.

Nevertheless, Ogilvie Homes, a Stirling-based house builder, was said to be interested and the provisional sale of the ground to them, for £1.3m subject to planning permission, was announced before the start of the 2004/5 season – never good for morale.

Many fans began to do their sums and worked out that if that sum were to be divided among shareholders based on their holding, the combined board would receive around £1.2m. The remainder of the stakeholders, to paraphrase Anne Robinson, would leave with next to nothing.

The most urgent question for the club's support was one that no-one on the board, Mackin included, seemed able or willing to answer: 'Where do East Stirlingshire play if they have no stadium?' There was a parallel south of the border – sort of. Arsenal, the English champions-elect at the time, were also on the move, to new premises designated as The Stadium. The Shire were heading for A Stadium, and no-one knew where, or when.

There had been talk of sharing with Falkirk FC in their new, council-owned arena on the outskirts of the town close to Grangemouth, or even on a rent-to-share basis with fellow Third Division side Stenhousemuir, a couple of miles down the road. Grangemouth Stadium, which had a presentable football pitch in the middle of its athletics track, had also been mentioned.

But a move anywhere would probably involve another change in name and the club's groundswell support would not countenance that. As one Shire fan told me: 'They have been East Stirlingshire for an awful long time. I, for one, am not suddenly going to start supporting a club called Grangemouth United. I'm from Falkirk and this is the only club in the town. I don't count Falkirk FC any longer. They're in Grangemouth now as far as we are concerned.'

The genuine fear of most Shire fans was that Mackin and the board would simply sell up, walk away, and allow the club to join the ranks of other vanished Scottish football institutions like Third Lanark, Clydebank and Airdrieonians. They were determined not to allow this to happen and, as their forerunners in the Steedman era had done, they mobilised.

They set up a self-funded trust in an effort to have more say in the running of the club and even wrote to the SFL demanding an inquiry because they felt the board – based on Mackin's infamous decision in the summer of 2002 to set a wage cap of £10 a week and his lack of investment in Firs Park – was deliberately setting the club out to be uncompetitive.

Mackin's famous wage cut had made national news, along with what amounted to a mass walk-out of senior players with their eyes on their mortgage or their next trip to Malaga. The letter to the SFL, who probably receive several hundred a year from disaffected fans complaining about various football boards, went unacknowledged and at the height of the furore the SFL presented the Shire with even more disturbing news: they would consider forcing a club that finished bottom in successive seasons to seek re-election.

There could only have been one candidate in mind. Then, as now, there was no relegation from the Third Division and the Shire, despite their appalling playing record, had enjoyed this feudal right, untroubled by the prospect of playing in the Highland League, or the West of Scotland Super League, for most of their history.

The Shire fans and board were still taking in the prospect of summary execution when UEFA, via the SFA, struck another blow. All Scottish senior football grounds, from the 2005/6 season, said the SFA, would have to be of a minimum size. The recommended criteria added up to 105 metres long and 68 metres wide. The Firs Park pitch measured 99 by 65. Jimmy Wilson's £200 budget would plainly be stretched to its limit.

The problems mounted. The SFA announced, almost in the same breath, that henceforth all head coaches and assistants should possess a coaching certificate. Neither the Shire's

current head coach, nor his assistant, possessed paper qualifications and the SFA's preliminary award could only be
earned after a course costing £495. This amounted to the
club's monthly electricity or gas bill. The board decided that
their budgetary priorities lay elsewhere.

All these fiscal problems were good news for me, of course.
They strengthened my case. For two grand the club could
invest in a ton of grass seed, paint new white lines, send
their staff on numerous coaching courses and still have
enough left over to replenish the boardroom optics.

Alan J. Mackin, however, had his own agenda. He led me
into the Portakabin labelled Boardroom, handed me a can
of unchilled Irn-Bru (the optics on the corner bar were
indeed empty) and I sat down opposite the assembled mind-
ers of East Stirlingshire FC.

They were a prototype of every football club board in
history. The hard-case chairman was on my left, pouring
over my written proposal. The genial secretary/chief execu-
tive/manager sat opposite, pen poised over the minutes.
There was a large overweight man with a jolly red face, and
a small aggressive pensioner in his seventies. These two sat
slightly apart from a fastidious-looking man with a hearing
aid and another, in his late thirties, who sat through the
proceedings in silence.

The pensioner was clearly Alex Forsyth, the king of the
veto; the ruddy-faced man, his son-in-law, John Morton.
Alec McCabe, said to be the financial mastermind, was the
dainty one with hearing difficulties and Douglas Morrison,
a Dumbarton schoolteacher, the mute.

We waited for Mackin to finish reading and I took in the
interior of the East Stirlingshire bunker. The trophy cabinet
contained three pieces of unpolished silverware. The lettering
on one of them read 'Stirlingshire Cup 2000, Winners East

Stirlingshire FC'. Another identical but slightly more tarnished trophy was for winning the same competition in 1969. The lettering on the other was hidden under a layer of brown oxide, but I assumed it was the Second Division trophy, *circa* 1931/2. Some tattered club pennants, like the heads of slaughtered big game, were impaled on the wall by drawing pins.

The Formica-topped table around which we were all seated was square, highlighting the divide between Forsyth/Morton and the others. Like most of the Shire working areas, it was a room so musty it looked as though it had sprouted its own furniture and the carpet was heavily stained with countless spilt drinks – the legacy of a thousand post-match wakes.

Mackin spoke: 'Jeff, I like you, you're a nice guy, but two grand isn't enough. We have people interested in this club. A TV company wants to come down and film us for the season and the newspapers and radio are queuing up to get involved. We are becoming famous.' I blinked and looked round the table. Thomson was smiling into his minutes. McCabe watched me intently. Morton kept his head down.

The septuagenarian chimed in: 'Did you know Alex Ferguson was here?' The others ignored him. Morton smiled indulgently. Mackin gave my proposal a backhand smash, like a KGB interrogator whose impatience is wearing thin, and spoke again: 'Two grand? That's an insult.'

'Well, that's all I've got.'

'We're not going to do it for that.'

Mackin leafed through my proposal again, I re-examined the trophy cabinet and took a sip of the Irn-Bru.

McCabe cleared his throat and suggested a compromise: £2,000 up front and a share of the royalties to the club and I could have all the access I liked. I could even come back as a guest at another board meeting. This seemed reasonable, particularly as on that basis I felt I could write exactly what I liked, particularly about those board meetings.

'What about the manager?' I asked finally. 'Will you clear it with him?' Mackin looked at Les Thomson, Thomson looked at Mackin, then at me. 'I told you,' said Thomson, 'he's the coach. I'm the manager here.'

'I know Sir Alex Ferguson,' said Forsyth.

I made my excuses and left. I was in, at a price. But into what?

Outside, a man in his early fifties, dressed in a smart, navy-blue business suit, packet of Hamlet cigars in one hand and mobile phone in the other, was passing on his way out of the ground. 'I'm Dennis Newall,' he said. 'I'm the manager here.'

2

MASSACRE AT THE
HOUSE OF THE BLUE TOON

===

If football judges managerial success on a complicated equation involving a club's history, resources, level of expectation and support, then Dennis Newall – or any Shire manager for that matter – must be considered a success. If only for the ability to get eleven starters and five subs on the park every Saturday.

East Stirlingshire have a history all right, but in over a century of effort they have mustered few honours to put on a roll. They had been Division Two champions (in 1931/2) and won the Stirlingshire Cup twice. They had beaten Celtic in a five-a-side match in 1963 and had the pictures of a crestfallen Bobby Lennox coming off the Brockville pitch to prove it. Sir Alex Ferguson, as everyone very kindly, and frequently, reminded me, *was* there for a time, as were the Scottish internationals Eddie McCreadie, later of Chelsea, and George Wood, who moved to Blackpool for £10,000. The club had also picked up a record £35,000 when they sold striker Jim Docherty, again to Chelsea. But that was about it.

As for resources, level of expectation and support, forget it. Mackin's ordinance on the first was well chronicled, the only expectation was that they would lose by humiliating margins every week and the average home gate was around 200. But Dennis Newall did have one thing in his favour and when things got sticky for him in the months ahead, as they did many times, I could justifiably tell the manager of the least successful football team in British football: 'You must have the safest job in the game.'

'How's that?'

'Because no-one else is daft enough to do it.'

When Steve Morrison, Newall's predecessor, quit in February 2004 – his assistant Alex Cleland, having seen the light a month earlier, had already left to join the coaching staff at Partick Thistle (if that can be regarded as seeing the light) – Newall had been on a shortlist of two as a potential replacement. And he played a blinder at the interview. 'I'll do the job for nothing,' he told the board. No contest. Looking back, I could picture the gleam in Mackin's eye. The vote for him was unanimous. Even Alex Forsyth, the Nikita Khrushchev of the Shire Security Council, decided to forego his traditional right of veto.

Newall, who drove a BMW 3 Series and was a sales director for a hydraulic engineering company, plainly didn't need a job which some had likened to the labour of Sisyphus, the poor unfortunate in Greek mythology who, having upset the gods, was sentenced to push a large rock uphill for eternity. Newall wanted a foot on the Division managers' ladder but his inheritance was dubious, to say the least. When he arrived at Firs Park, the club were closing in fast on an unwanted record – that of the worst campaign in British senior football since Glasgow's defunct Abercorn Rovers lost twenty-four straight games in the season of 1897. And that is going back a long way. The Shire had one win to their name – against Elgin City at Firs Park back in November 2003. That was to be followed by twenty-three successive defeats.

Such ineptitude attracted what any manager would

describe as the wrong sort of headlines. On their home patch, week after week, the *Falkirk Herald*'s sub-editors would struggle to come up with something original to go above the Shire match reports. In the end, they had to settle for the blindingly obvious: 'Shire make bottom spot their own'; 'More heartbreak for Shire'; 'Shire snatch defeat from the jaws of victory – again'; 'Hopeless Shire sinking'; 'Another chance slips by for Shire'. The Scottish tabloids were more pointed: 'What a bag of Shire', wrote the *Scottish Sun*.

The Shire were big news abroad. In Holland the side's deeds, or rather misdeeds, featured regularly in *De Telegraaf* and *AD Sportwereld*. They also featured occasionally in *L'Equipe* and *La Gazzetta dello Sport*. Other newspapers round the world offered regular reports couched in the terms of a weekly medical bulletin.

Back home, the media was beating down Les Thomson's door to get a slant on what it meant to be involved with the worst team in Britain. When Arsenal were in sight of the Premier League title early in 2004, Radio Five Live even tried to set up a phone link-up between Thomson and his Highbury counterpart David Dein. Dein was agreeable but Thomson, who at that time was not into marketing the hopelessness of his club, wasn't going to buy that one. 'Don't you think I know what you're at?' he demanded of the Five Live researcher. 'You're only interested because we haven't won a game for months!' The show's producer had to agree that this, indeed, was the case and the project was shelved.

So predictable were Saturdays with the Shire that the pools companies had removed their name from the fixed odds coupon, along with the other punters' pal, Arsenal. The champions-elect had become unbackable because they won everything, the Shire unbackable because they lost everything

– together, they were the two stone-cold certainties in hundreds of accumulator bets.

The bookies were not best pleased and a spokesman for Ladbrokes said: 'East Stirlingshire are a tiny club but have already cost us millions this year. They are a banker on the coupon every week and more people back them to lose than Celtic to win. People from across the UK and the world are backing whoever plays against them. If they could win one more game this season, it would alleviate some of our losses.'

The Shire's ineptitude, however, did attract sympathy, and support of sorts. As the 2003/4 season wore on, and their plight worsened on and off the field, help arrived from some unlikely quarters.

Sir Alex Ferguson sent down some signed Manchester United jerseys for auction and the club began to earn the sort of backing that once belonged to other inhabitants of the sporting deep, such as ski-jumper Eddie 'The Eagle' Edwards and Eric 'The Eel' Moussambani, the Olympic swimmer from Equatorial Guinea. The Shire became cult heroes. People laughed at them, but in the admiring way that the British public, with their fondness for gentle lunacy, reserve for the truly hopeless-yet-plucky.

Fan clubs sprang up worldwide, announcing that the Shire 'are now our second club'; in addition to Coventry in England, Turkey, Australia and even Bulgaria had branches. In Holland, a Shire fan club attracted eleven members. But everyone knew that the Shire's global fame was based on their ignominy. This state of affairs, to some at least, was unacceptable.

When Dennis Newall took his seat in the manager's office, towards the end of March 2004, recovery looked an unlikely prospect. Six defeats on the trot, one a hurtful and 'fucking embarrassing' 8-1 loss at one of his former clubs, Albion

Rovers, took him to the last game of the season and within touching distance of joining the ill-fated Abercorn Rovers in the history books.

Elgin City, beaten (incredibly) at home earlier in the season when Steve Morrison was still in charge, were the visitors at Firs Park. On an afternoon of high emotion, the Shire dug deep and with the help of an opposition own goal, won 2-1. Abercorn's record was safe. For all the wrong reasons, the Shire got as much press as Celtic and Rangers that day. How the bookies must have regretted the decision to drop them from the fixed odds.

Elgin headed back to the north-east of Scotland to reflect on the most unwanted soubriquet in British sport: in the space of 180 dreadful minutes they had become the Fall Guys for East Stirlingshire FC.

But the Shire were still rooted to the bottom of the Scottish Third Division, still a pub joke. I wondered why players would be willing to turn out for them and subject themselves to almost universal ridicule. I wondered why a manager would take on a job that paid nothing, with a playing staff earning next to nothing, at a club who were winning nothing.

Newall had laid his cards on the table from the start. He had ambition. 'It was a job I had always wanted,' he told me. 'I had applied three times, and felt an affiliation to the club having played here. It's challenging taking on a small club, with a decent set-up and it's worth having a go at it. It's a case of starting at the bottom to work your way up. I look at East Stirling as a stepping stone. How many people would like this job? Half a million, I'd say.

'What I want now is some sort of success on the park. The ideal scenario is us sitting mid-table and some players getting noticed and maybe moving for money. If we make a success of it, the money would fall into place somewhere else. We may get a reward somewhere else. If we can succeed with the resources we have here, other clubs may sit up and take notice.'

He was also keen to get a place on what he described as 'Scottish football's managerial merry-go-round'. Famous former players like Billy Stark of Queen's Park, Davie Hay then at Dunfermline (though not for much longer) and Sandy Clark of Berwick Rangers (also shortly heading for pastures new) never seemed to experience any difficulty picking up a new club, even after being dismissed from their old one.

There was also what amounted to a cadre of established managers who had done the rounds at various Scottish clubs and were employed on what amounted to a rotation basis. 'It's a lot easier if you are in that circle,' pointed out Newall. 'Some of these guys will never be out of a job. I have to earn my Brownie points here. But I do have the hunger and desire to succeed.'

On paper at least, some of his players possessed the same hopes and desires. At the start of the season I had circulated some pro-forma questionnaires. I only got half a dozen completed ones back – they are footballers, after all – but some of these were illuminating.

Alongside the statutory questions such as favourite film (*Shawshank Redemption* was the overwhelming No.1), favourite TV programme (*Only Fools and Horses*) and who would you most like to be trapped in a lift with (Abi Titmuss), I had asked: Ambition in football? One player, who wasn't even a regular starter at the time, replied: 'To play for my country'. Another, asked how he handled mates in the pub who laughed at the Shire, responded: 'I ask how many of them are playing senior football'. And for all their low level of achievement, the Shire are senior football.

Scotland has a thriving junior set-up, noted mainly for the unbridled ferocity of its play and the funding the clubs can generate – most have flourishing social clubs and backing from local business. Officially amateur, they can offer players a healthy remuneration, or living expenses. The Shire lost a goalkeeper before the start of the 2004/5 season when a junior side offered him £5,500 to take a step down. These clubs, the likes of Sauchie Juniors, Cumbernauld United and Gala Fairydean, also have better facilities than the Shire, but to Dennis Newall the goalie was simply demonstrating a lack of ambition.

More tellingly, junior matches seldom attract league scouts and their match reports never appear in the newspapers. Players at Shotts Bon Accord can't read their personal man-by-man ratings in the *Sunday Mail*, or the *Sunday Post*; Shire players can – and most of them do. Whatever the reality, the potential fame and (lack of) fortune in senior football is clearly a heady lure.

In his subterranean office, with its fine view of the back of the dugouts and Jimmy Wilson's legs going about their daily business, Newall's in-tray was stacked with handwritten notes from what he called 'no-account wankers'. The letters, some pleading for a trial, others demanding a game, came mainly from teenagers – or their fathers. Sometimes their mothers. He gave most of them short shrift.

On my first visit there, Newall took a call from – let's call him Patrick – of County Clare, in the Republic of Ireland. Patrick didn't care about the £10-a-week wages, the fact that he would have to pay his own way over, the prospect of finding a job in Falkirk (current unemployment level: sixteen per cent) or even where he would live. The Shire would be his opportunity for fame and fortune. But this was no Roy Keane, or Damien Duff:

'Hello there, is that the manager?'

'Aye, I'm Dennis Newall.'

'I want to sign for you.'

'Wait a minute, what position do you play?'

'Well, I'm sort of a utility player.'

'I asked, where do you play?'

'I'm a goalkeeper . . . or right-side midfielder.'

Newall's office is a time capsule, unchanged since the days when Alex Ferguson sat there and thought dark thoughts about the directors next door. There is a filing cabinet in one corner which the manager claims he never uses. 'I've never even looked inside,' he said. 'It may be full of cans of Tennents for all I know.'

Close to an unframed aerial photograph of the ground, above him and to his left an ancient wall-mounted extractor fan does its best to deal with his exhaled Hamlet smoke. The carpet is worn and stained and he conducts business from behind the standard Formica-topped desk with his scribbled list of playing staff, ashtray, two mobile phones – one for business, one for the club – and his cheap cigars. A dark suit usually hangs on a peg in the corner, there's a blue kit bag on the floor with the logo Buildbase and there is, always, a lingering smell of liniment mingled with the smell of stale cigar smoke. It is the odour of football.

In the good old days, of course, managers' careers ended when they died of old age. Now they are at the mercy of results. A career can be over as a result of one moment of indecision, or ineptitude, on the pitch. And in the good old days, the manager picked the team and left everything else to a trainer; now he has to be mother, father, psychologist – and in the case of many players in Scotland, psychiatrist, too. A nasty streak helps – because eventually every player

Top: The stresses and strains of management: Dennis Newall goes through the wringer.

Previous page: 'This is Firs Park'. The players' and directors' entrance.

Below: The main stand at Firs Park: it's a tight squeeze – in the dug-out at least.

Food glorious food: the
Shire pie shop. After the
dispute was resolved,
obviously.

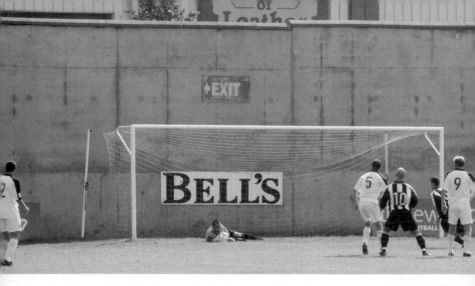

The Gretna goalkeeper saves; the Land of Leather wall watches.

Above: David Harvey delivers, watched by Chris Newall.

Left: Jamie Dunbar: gone but not forgotten.

Right: Alex Forsyth and son-in-law John Morton watch in splendid isolation.

Middle: Chris Baldwin, Ross Donaldson, Chris Miller and Paul Ross in the thick of things against Gretna. Derek Townsend is on the right.

Bottom: Ross Donaldson accelerates into ramming speed.

Top: In the House of Blue Toon: like penguins on a shore infested by killer whales.

The tractors' graveyard: Central Park, Cowdenbeath.

Bottom: Rowan Alexander, left, discusses tactics in front of the Shire boardroom.

Top: The Shire's financial mastermind Alec McCabe with the silent Douglas Morrison.

Right: The author does his best Jose Mourinho impression alongside Greig Denham, while, top to bottom, Chris Baldwin, Derek Rae and The Cat wonder when they will get some playing time.

Bottom: All hands to the pumps: Laura Gillogley, Jimmy Wilson and Bobby Jack give Paul Ross a lift. Was he felled by one of his manager's verbal assaults?

Fame and fortune beckoned one lucky player.

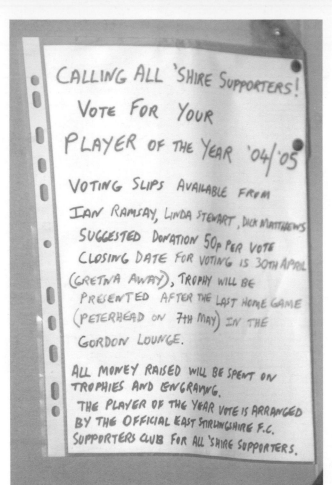

CALLING ALL 'SHIRE SUPPORTERS!
VOTE FOR YOUR
PLAYER OF THE YEAR '04/'05

VOTING SLIPS AVAILABLE FROM
IAN RAMSAY, LINDA STEWART, DICK MATTHEWS
SUGGESTED DONATION 50p PER VOTE
CLOSING DATE FOR VOTING IS 30TH APRIL
(GRETNA AWAY), TROPHY WILL BE
PRESENTED AFTER THE LAST HOME GAME
(PETERHEAD ON 7TH MAY) IN THE
GORDON LOUNGE.

ALL MONEY RAISED WILL BE SPENT ON
TROPHIES AND ENGRAVING.
THE PLAYER OF THE YEAR VOTE IS ARRANGED
BY THE OFFICIAL EAST STIRLINGSHIRE F.C.
SUPPORTERS CLUB FOR ALL 'SHIRE SUPPORTERS.

He might have missed out to Derek Ure on the vote, but Scott Livingston (below) had his fans. The Coventry Branch of the Supporters Club voted him their Player of the Year. It is unclear how many games they attended.

is going to be told he is no longer good enough – as does an ability to treat every player as an individual. He has to know when to kick and when to cuddle.

A modern-day manager has to deal with boards of directors, many of whose knowledge of the modern game is sketchy to say the least and who remain convinced that a player with No. 11 on his back is automatically marked by an opposing player wearing the No. 2 jersey. Many fans, more preoccupied with what a player does on the ball rather than what he does off it, will be convinced that they could do a far better job and usually say so. Whether they would relish the stress and strains which go with the territory is open to question.

Newall holds down a full-time job and is also at Firs Park three times a week, twice for training and once for a match. He is at some sort of football match most nights to scout possible new talent. His monthly mobile bills on Shire business, he says, amount to around £600. Like many managers, aware perhaps of the old adage that 'players win matches, managers lose them', he would rather still be out on the park.

As a player, he had operated mainly in the junior ranks, with professional spells at Stranraer and the Shire. He went back to the juniors before returning to Firs Park in the 1986/7 season. He didn't get a first-team game, as some of his players liked to remind themselves behind his back. Like Ferguson's, Rafael Benitez's and Jose Mourinho's, et al., careers, Newall's playing career had been moderate, but: 'One thing I gave was commitment. I didn't have a lot of skill, more the headless chicken syndrome, but I did have a physical presence. What do you weigh? Around fourteen stone? I could put you through that wall.

'It really frustrates me that some of the boys at the Shire

have talent I didn't have and don't apply it. Firs Park hasn't changed much since I was here. The grass is a bit longer. The results haven't changed much either.

'After I retired as a player my boy Chris was playing for Celtic North Boys' Club and I would go along and watch. Then I got to help out with the coaching. One day I met the secretary of Cumbernauld United in a shopping mall. They were managerless and he asked me if I fancied having a go. I was there four-and-a-half years and in the season we won the league we lost only two games. It was a good period. I didn't spend much money on players, maybe a thousand pounds in that time, but it taught me about juggling the books.

'Management is a learning curve, you try and head in an upwards direction. From Cumbernauld I went to Albion Rovers as reserve team coach with Bobby Russell. Then I had three years as their commercial manager, doing the billboards, the programmes, everything. But I was missing the management side, so I took on Lesmahagow Juniors, and here I am today.'

At Cumbernauld, Newall had managed to impose some discipline on a pretty undisciplined bunch by adopting what he saw as a professional approach. The players had to arrive before a game in suit and tie; those who didn't were fined. Players who believed they had a divine right to play every weekend found themselves warming the bench. He perfected what he called the paint-stripping treatment in the dressing room, a series of Ferguson-style rants that he would use to even greater, and louder, effect at Firs Park.

'I have been assembling guys at East Stirling who probably weren't good enough somewhere else,' he told me, with memorable understatement. 'Talking to them in a sensible quiet manner just won't work. If that has to be paint stripping, so be it. No one goes out on the park to play badly, but you can talk to them all day long and you have to rule by fear. I don't like paint stripping, but if we start getting points there might be a different approach. I'm not there to be liked and if they go out saying "stuff him" so be it. I am quite hard on a lot of them but if I just sit back and accept it I'll be dead.'

Dennis Newall is fond of comparing himself to TV's *X-Factor* hatchet man Simon Cowell in that he has to be cruel to be kind. 'Some of them don't expect anything else,' he explained. 'The ones I think have talent, who can do a job for us, I give it to them all the time.'

It is unlikely, however, that Simon Cowell ever called someone a fucking c**t to their faces in front of a roomful of others. Most of the Shire players, it must be said, never batted an eyelid. They seemed to take it as a birthright.

Pre-season, Newall had got rid of some dead wood, signed six new players and mixed and matched with the leftovers from the season from hell. The incomers were drawn mainly from the amateur ranks or were discards from other Third Division sides. The old guard, as he liked to call them, were there to make up the numbers.

Four of them, he insisted when we spoke that summer, 'should not be here at all'. Given the choice, he would have got rid of them, too, but he needed the numbers. As he pointed out, some of these players had become so inured to the prospect of heavy defeat that they almost expected it by right. A goal against was the equivalent of a puppy being shown a slipper. They would subside into snivelling sub-servience against the feeblest of opposition.

In early July, the traditional rituals of pre-season began. Players straggled back from Torremolinos and Playa das Americas with San Miguel paunches and orange faces, ready to embark on a punishing training regime designed to bring them to peak fitness for the season ahead – in other words, a few trots round the local park.

The traditional opening friendlies brought a 4–0 defeat by Premier League Livingston and a 1–0 defeat to Clyde, both at Firs Park. The Livingston defeat was predictable, as was the reaction of some of the football aristocrats to the Shire's changing quarters. The Spaniard Oscar Rubio, who had once been on the books of Real Madrid and, one suspects, had been used to better things at the Bernabeu, complained that the water in the shower was too hot, surely a first in football at any level. Another emerged from the away dressing room muttering about 'a shite-hole'.

Then the problems began. With two more pre-season games scheduled, against Cumbernauld United and Arbroath, towards the end of July, the Firs Park centre circle was suddenly infested by a swarm of giant flies attracted by the flourishing grass, the prolific weeds and, maybe, the smell of failure. It became a no-go area for anyone dressed in shorts.

This, according to the club at any rate, was the reason both fixtures were switched to Grangemouth Stadium. The Shire support, always prone to conspiracy theories, suspected it wasn't so much a case of grassy centre circle, as grassy knoll. They had an alternative explanation: if the board was about to sell Firs Park and move house then this was a preliminary, and none-too-subtle, attempt to familiarise everyone with their new surroundings. Mackin remained silent on the issue.

Built by British Petroleum as 'a means of giving something back to the town' (those locals who fear the prospect of major environmental damage are thus rendered impotent by the notion of smiling benefaction), Grangemouth Stadium fronts the *Blade Runner*-like skyline of the oil refinery's steaming cooling towers and vertical piping which belch fire and fumes into the Grangemouth sky.

Bobby Jack, the part-time ground help at Firs Park, spent a large part of his working life there, and claims that they like to get rid of 'the really shite stuff' during the night. The company has been fined several times for environmental abuse, but at least the area's young athletes have inherited the means to breathe in the miasma more quickly and more efficiently. The stadium boasts field event areas, a floodlit running track and, in the middle distance, a full-sized football pitch.

I arrived to find fourteen fans in the grandstand, along with a lone journalist. Tadek Kopszywa, known as Tad, had been condemned by fate to follow the Shire home and away. He has a withered arm, a microphone attached to a tape recorder and an undisguised suspicion of outsiders. I asked if he worked for the local paper, the *Falkirk Herald*. 'Na,' he replied. 'I dinnae work for them, I just write for them.'

Tad, who has a peculiar habit when excited of ducking his head to his waist and spinning his whole upper torso from the hips, is a man of many parts. Shire correspondent for the *Falkirk Herald*, local radio reporter and a Shire shareholder, he also contributes to the match programme and sits on the committee of the fans' trust. And he was Jimmy Wilson's co-manager on their glorious, two-game, unbeaten run.

The objects of our affections were seated in an unenthusiastic circle in the middle of the park. 'This is Jeff,' said Dennis Newall. 'He's here to write a book about youse.' The players looked, if anything, even more unenthusiastic, staring at me like the children in *Village of the Damned*.

I took stock and attempted to put names to faces and jobs to names. All, save the odd unemployed player and student, had day jobs, some of them surprisingly cerebral. There was the inevitable postman and a plumber. Graham McGhee, captain at the time, was a cooper, and subject to the predictable leg-pulling about 'barrel of laughs' or 'he ain't got a barrel of money'. But Tony Mitchell, the goal-keeper, was an architect, Sean McAuley, a crew-cutted mid-fielder, a dealer for an investment company, and Jamie McKay, a stocky defender, worked in insurance. Scott Livingstone, the club's most consistent performer and prob-ably its swiftest, was a surveyor.

We also had a journalist, Gordon Parks, who wrote about football for the *Daily Record*. The newspaper and the club had also agreed that he could chronicle the fortunes of a season of the Shire in a Monday sports column – a decision that was to cause him, his newspaper and the club a lot of angst later.

The Norwegian midfielder, the Shire's first foreign player, was easily recognisable. Carl Erich Thywissen had a day job with Shell Finance, dressed in Harvey Nichols' best, and had arrived with a statuesque and very blonde Swedish girlfriend called Johanna. He also spoke better English than most of his new team-mates and plainly didn't need the tenner a week.

It turned out he had actually been born in Leicester. He had been at university with Scott Livingstone, who had per-suaded him to come and give the Shire a try. With his long face, straggling beard and expression of continual bemuse-ment, he resembled Scooby-Doo's hairy wee pal, and was, unsurprisingly, christened Shaggy. Given that he cost nothing and is paid virtually nothing, Thywissen is arguably the best foreign import, pound for pound, in Scottish football.

His Shire career did not get off to a good start, however. Newall, who dislikes any show of what he sees as ostentation, didn't like Shaggy's Beckham-esque patented silver boots and ordered him to change them. Twenty minutes into the game, the Scandinavian tweaked a hamstring.

Laura Gillogley, the Shire physio, was adamant that the player would be up and running before the season proper, but she had reckoned without the Curse of the Shire. The club had forgotten that Norway is not in the EU ('Why the fuck not? Everyone else up there is.') and had failed to apply for a work visa. Condemned to the sidelines, Shaggy's long face grew even more lugubrious.

The 4-0 victory at Grangemouth, over admittedly light-weight Cumbernauld opposition, produced some positive signs as the new season approached. The Shire No. 10, Jamie Dunbar, scored twice and was unquestionably the man of the match. Dunbar, however, was on the books of the junior side Cumnock United, who were driving a hard bargain. They wanted £2,000 for him. 'Two grand? I could buy the fucking stadium for that,' said Newall. 'Where do they think they're coming from?'

His other new signings looked promising. A four-square striker called Ross Donaldson who, with his shaven head, unshaven chin and belligerent outlook resembled a 1970s French rugby hooker, put himself about in no uncertain fashion. Donaldson had arrived from the exotically named Rutherglen Glencairn, but there was nothing exotic about his game.

He spat, he swore, he pushed, he poked. His broad beam made it virtually impossible to dispossess him, and he worked well with his back to goal – other players feeding off his flicks and stabs. He was what I recognise as an old-fashioned centre-forward, but already he was finding it hard to impress his new manager, who wasn't one for keeping his views to himself.

'Ross Donaldson and Burger King, a marriage made in heaven,' says Newall. 'Ross, your work-rate is shite.' 'Ross, you're not chasing back.' 'Ross, you're going to have to work on your fitness.' 'Ross, you couldn't trap a medicine ball.' And, from time to time: 'Ross you are a fucking disgrace.' The opposing centre-half called him a 'fat c∗∗t'.

Amazingly, the delivery driver from Bellshill took all this without a murmur, although I spent much of the season wondering where, and when, he would finally crack and turn on his tormentors. Even I could see that if Donaldson was to lose weight he would lose his main strength – the inability of the opposition to get round him to the ball.

Newall has a fine line in abusive rhetoric and, like many football managers, possesses the characteristics of a school-teacher – sarcastic, sceptical, occasionally caustic and capable of exaggeration. He is both seer and jester. 'Shaggy, you've got a head like a three-penny bit, or a crown, or a kroner, or whatever you have back home,' he told the bemused Norwegian.

Donaldson apart, the manager's favoured target for abuse was a diminutive midfielder from Glasgow called Paul Ross. Newall doesn't like Paul Ross's suntan, this being evidence of an ego that he believes could drag the club down – 'he thinks he has arrived because he is playing for us.' Ross had been with Newall at Albion Rovers and, like many protégés, seemed to attract an unreasonable amount of criticism.

The new manager's team talks were carefully choreo-graphed to incorporate a stylised rant about his own side and the opposition, some tactical promptings, a tentative look ahead at the next fixture and, finally, a step aside to allow his assistant, Greig Denham, his moment. 'Greig?' he'd say.

Newall and Denham have been friends a long time and

there is a conspiratorial intimacy between them endemic to most double acts. There is also the good cop, bad cop element. Newall questions his players' manhood, batters them, knocks them to the ground. Denham picks them up, dusts them down, and tells them how they can do better. By midseason, however, Denham's good cop had metamorphosised into a pretty fearsome bad cop. Smiling encouragement simply would not work with a defence that was losing three goals a game and an attack that was almost toothless.

Denham didn't have the manager's gift for metaphor-laden eloquence, but as a player who was once on the books of Motherwell, St Mirren and Falkirk, he arguably commanded more respect. At twenty-eight, he was also of the same generation as the players. Tall, around 6 foot 2 inches, and with an obvious wiry strength, his career had been almost destroyed by injury.

Aged sixteen, he had been signed by the then Motherwell manager Tommy McLean and had looked a fine prospect, strong in the tackle and dominant in the air. He had a spell with Cumbernauld, where he had first met Newall, and was voted their young player of the year. At Motherwell, he had played under Alex McLeish and alongside the likes of the late Davie Cooper, Brian Martin and Lee McCulloch who was helping Wigan win promotion to the English Premier League. Denham had progressed in the opposite direction.

McLeish released him at the end of the 1999/2000 season, St Mirren did likewise in the summer of 2003. He joined Arbroath, and then picked up a cruciate ligament injury which looked as though it might end his career. The surgeon advised him to retire. Like many footballers, however, he refused to lie down and six operations later he was back training – with Albion Rovers. He returned to Cumbernauld and was then persuaded by Newall to take on a player–coach job at the Shire. It was his first shot at this sort of thing.

Denham addressed the players as 'lads' and the 'lads' listened attentively. Kenny Quinn, the deputy assistant coach, and another ex-pro – who was to depart mid-season allegedly upset that he couldn't get a game – seldom got a word in. 'It's my man-management and Greig's coaching know-how, that's how it works,' explained Dennis. 'We are a package.'

Well, it worked against the juniors of Cumbernauld, although even to my unpractised eye, the Shire's limitations were plain. Their captain and longest-serving player, McGhee, or Gee as he is known, had the look of the sax player in *The Commitments* and played with the same dainty fastidiousness. Like the other Shire players he inherited, Newall had little patience with Gee. 'He's a nice guy, but being a nice guy doesn't make you a nice footballer,' he said.

The two full-backs, Chris Miller and David Harvey, were solid enough, and there was a fair-haired winger called Chris Baldwin who possessed pace and balance on the ball but who fell over a lot in tackles and seemed too willing to blame team-mates when things went wrong. The back four was marshalled by Chris Newall, raw-boned and competitive. Chris is the son of the manager, which begged the obvious question, but his father insisted: 'Oh aye, I get asked that all the time and so does he. But in the dressing room now I can be on his case. He's no different from anyone else if he fucks up.'

Chris had been to Firs Park as a toddler when his father played there. 'We had a communal bath installed,' Dennis Newall recalled. 'Chris used to come along to training nights. After training I was in the bath with the other players and then went out to find Christopher crying because he couldn't get in with us. I still give him a bit of stick about that eighteen years on. Now he's back here as a man.'

McKay, another survivor of the pre-season cull and another Newall target, completed the back four. Up front, Donaldson held the ball up well and scored a fine goal. The 4–0 win at Grangemouth was a rare clean sheet at any level and the club's two goalkeepers, who played a half each, were hardly troubled.

Are all goalkeepers mad? It is a clichéd question, but to want to play between the sticks for the Shire . . . surely you have to be? The acknowledged Shire No. 1, Mitchell, is known as The Cat. This probably started off as heartless irony, a laddish leg-pull after some major gaffe, but like many nicknames it has stuck. Even Mitchell calls himself The Cat: 'Cat's ball,' he would shout when coming out to take a cross.

Six feet tall and weighing in at over 14 stone, The Cat possessed the traditional physical attributes of most keepers, and the same eccentricities. Before any match, he would wind himself up in alarming fashion, rolling his shoulders and smacking fist into palm, like a boxer. He insisted on playing the theme from *Rocky* on his ghetto blaster before a match. 'Come ooaan, the Shire,' he'd bawl. 'Winners, eh?'

Unfortunately for a management whose main attacking ploy revolves round the keeper booting the ball high into opposition territory in the hope of finding the head of one of his midfielders, or engendering an error in the opposition – all good stuff – there was one drawback: The Cat couldn't kick a dead ball for toffee. This was a big, big problem because most players at this level don't have the ability to play the ball sweetly out of defence; mainly because at this level no-one gets any time on the ball. Those wide open spaces seen at Hampden or the Bernabeu don't exists in the Scottish Third Division; every throw-in, every pass, every tackle is fiercely contested. Most players at this level possess physical commitment. Few possess skill.

The Cat could kick in the warm-ups all right, but a psychological block seemed to descend upon him in match situations. He could be a great shot-stopper, but most of the time he struggled to get the ball to halfway with his dead-ball kicks. Playing into the wind at Grangemouth, one of his spooned clearances was caught mid-flight and almost carried back over his head for an own goal. The Cat became his own shot-stopper.

The Cumbernauld keeper, by contrast, almost scored direct from a goalkick. Ross Gilpin, the other Shire keeper, was very young and had a kick like a mule. He had both timing and accuracy. But he is small, and wasn't in The Cat's class when it came to making saves. I sensed a managerial dilemma there.

Five days later we were back at Grangemouth, this time to see Arbroath's youth team take a 2-0 lead only for the Shire to reply with four of their own. Eight goals in two matches, this was heady stuff, but we all knew the real test would come on the following Saturday, when Second Division Berwick Rangers arrived at Firs Park for the first home game proper.

A good cup run, as in 'the league's gone but hopefully we can have a good cup run', is the fantasy of every manager, every player, every fan, but most of all for every club treasurer. The Shire were eligible for four; in ascending order of importance the Stirlingshire Cup, the Bell's Cup, the CIS Cup and the Scottish Cup – but realistically only the first offered any prospect of success. Even then they would have to contrive a way past their high-flying local rivals, Falkirk.

Peterhead away in the CIS Cup and the next game at home to Berwick Rangers in the Bell's Cup already had the look of lost causes. As for the Scottish Cup, the SFL's faith in the Shire progressing in the country's most illustrious knock-out competition was probably best illustrated by the official fixture list which scheduled a league match on every Scottish Cup date after the third round.

The Berwick match was also my first chance to see the inside of the Firs Park dressing room on a working day. When I had told friends that I would be privy to the innermost workings of a league club dressing room, they had been mightily impressed. Men friends who were also football fans told me: 'God, you'll hear all the tactics, all the repartee. I wish I could have your job.' Female friends who were not football fans said: 'God, you'll get to see all those dicks. Why can't I have your job?' But glamorous it was not.

Where to put myself? I obviously couldn't sit down as the players were packed like sardines round the three walls, facing the fourth where the manager and his assistant stood. One vantage point was right by a washing machine and next to the toilets. But as I had to move aside constantly as a succession of nervous players emptied their bladders, and as the washing machine was churning loudly through its cycles, this did not prove to be position A. Instead, I shuffled across a floor covered in water bottles, kit bags and stocking tie-ups and stood in the showers.

The home dressing room was about ten feet square and decorated with a *Sun* newspaper calendar open to display the charms of Miss July. 'Laura' shared her wall with a note from the Scottish Footballers Provident Association (SPFA) reminding players of the perils of under-insurance, a clock in the shape of a football and a line of ancient team sheets.

The players sat in a carefully observed team order – the goalkeeper on the left all the way round to No. 11 at the other end – and looked and listened intently as their manager moved a team of black counters up and down a white, magnetised board in the shape of a football field, his tactical observations in direct competition with the rabble-rousing beat of The Cat's *Eye of the Tiger*, the flushing toilets and the vibratory screech of the washing machine by now on spin. Neither Dennis Newall nor Greig Denham could work out how to switch it off. In the end, Denham pulled out the plug at the wall. Greig had his say, then players got up and stomped around earnestly, high-fiveing each other and slapping backs. But it was all a bit too quiet.

Having played professional sport, I pride myself on recognising dressing room ambience, or lack of it, and it was all wrong here. The fierce war whoops on the other side of the wall easily drowned out the Shire's mutterings. Only The Cat, who despite his shortcomings in the kicking department had earned a start in goal, seemed ready. Eyes bulging and teeth clenched, he looked like an East German hammer thrower at the point of delivery.

Newall had a few final, man-to-man words for his burly striker, demanding that Ross Donaldson 'behave like an animal'. Donaldson, who plainly had no problems in this department, nodded and smiled a strangely menacing smile. 'Get your arse into gear and give that centre-half a hard time,' advised the manager. Donaldson nodded, and smiled again.

On the pitch he was marked by the Berwick captain, Mark Cowan, a veteran defender with flat feet and a lantern jaw. Cowan, who had played for Berwick as far back as 1994, had been immortalised in song by his fans. 'Oh, we ain't got a barrel of money, we've got Cowan and Vally', they had chanted during what everyone regarded as the club's golden era.

At Firs Park, a visiting fan informed me that Cowan ended most matches swathed in bloody bandages like Terry Butcher. I informed him in return that Ross Donaldson would probably do his best to maintain that tradition. 'Cows will have him for breakfast,' snorted the Berwick fan.

Donaldson is one of those players who manages to attract opprobrium from both home and away fans: 'get the chips out for the fat bastard', chanted the Berwick fans; 'think of tonight's curry', yelled the home support.

Berwick, as the flags of St George carried by their large, unruly support testified, actually play in England. Founded in the same year as the Shire, they had a somewhat more illustrious history, based in the main on a momentous day in January 1967, when they beat Rangers in the Scottish Cup. Not surprisingly, that had proved a hard act to follow and Berwick had remained rooted in the mid-to-lower regions of Scottish football ever since.

Until 2000, Firs Park had been a regular venue as The Borderers were stuck in the Third Division basement, but then they had won promotion to Division Two. They had moved on. Their fans greeted the appearance of the Shire with a rendition of *Walking in a Winter Wonderland*. Although, on close listening, the first word did, perhaps, sound more like 'wanking'.

Berwick's pedigree, and perhaps the expectations of their board, was to cost the manager in the dugout that day, Paul Smith, his job within a couple of months, infamously sacked in the car park at Stranraer after a 2–2 draw. His replacement would be former Hearts boss Sandy Clark, who had been on that much sought-after (in Dennis Newall's eyes anyway) merry-go-round of Scottish football clubs with jobs at Hearts, Hamilton Accies and St Johnstone. Latterly, he had been the Dunfermline strikers' coach and a BBC pundit.

At the end of the season, with Berwick relegated to Division Three and with the prospect of two more annual visits to Firs Park, and in advance of the dreaded vote of (no) confidence from the Berwick board, Clark himself was to jump ship and join the coaching staff at Aberdeen.

Smith was out of his dugout almost immediately as Donaldson and Cowan got stuck into each other. Here, the relevant tabloid jargon would read, 'it's the no-nonsense defender against a bustling striker'. A perhaps more accurate description would read, 'two dirty bastards kicking lumps out of each other'. There was a gladiatorial quality about the contest. Donaldson took Cowan's ankles away from behind, Cowan elbowed Donaldson in the face. But both climbed to their feet without a glance at the other, without recrimination – save the odd muttered imprecation – and trotted back to position ready for their next joust. The referee (shirt sponsor: Specsavers) either didn't notice the depravities of this 'scrap', or chose to turn a blind eye.

Within minutes, it became clear that the Land of Leather wall played a crucial role in any game at Firs Park. Standing only two yards from the goal line, it was an obvious hazard for a winger sprinting to the by-line. But it also severely limited the length of run-ups employed by goalkeepers taking by-kicks.

Teams who won the toss took little account of wind direction or slope of the pitch at Firs Park, preferring to condemn the opposing goalkeeper to the Land of Leather wall end for the first forty-five minutes and latch on to his half-hit clearances. If the wind was also against, a goalkeeper could struggle to get the ball out of his own penalty area.

It was a simple matter for a manager to defend a lead and run down the clock by ordering his troops to 'boot the fucking thing into the Land of Leather car park'. Visiting managers built their tactical master-plans around one of the UK's leading leather sofa retail specialists.

Pre-season, there had been desultory talk among the

coaching staff about the possibility of keeper Ross Gilpin – probably the club's best dead-ball kicker – taking free-kicks in match situations. Then Dennis Newall remembered the Land of Leather wall, the possibility of the opposing keeper being gifted the chance of a swift goal kick from a rebound and the sight of Gilpin stranded on the halfway line as a striker tapped the ball into an empty net. The idea was abandoned.

The Shire seem to be plagued by bad luck and, above all, irony. Berwick's first goal was scored by one of their former players and although Donaldson smashed in a glorious equaliser from thirty-five yards, a defensive lapse and a simple tap-in gave Berwick the victory. It was a result that seemed to leave both sides happy. The Shire avoided the expected drubbing and Berwick the ignominy of losing to them.

Smith criticised the playing surface, Newall restricted himself to reminding Donaldson about his waistline and Grant Findlay, a seventeen-year-old striker who had signed that morning, received a bollocking for signing autographs when he should have been warming up. But fame can go to anyone's head.

Outside, a bespectacled young home fan with the look of Piggy out of *Lord of the Flies* asked me for my autograph (the assumption was that anyone seated in the dugout must be a football celebrity). I put on my most indulgent smile, attempted to look as though this happened every day, and prepared to oblige. 'Are you the chairman?' asked Piggy.

One knockout competition down, three to go. The Shire had fallen at the first hurdle in the Bell's Cup with every likelihood that they would trip over the next, too. The SFA fixture computer had been uncommonly unkind coming up with opening league games scheduled against Third Division title favourites Peterhead and Gretna and a CIS Cup tie against Peterhead in between. This was also uncommonly unkind to the Shire's slender financial resources with the longest away trip, to the north-east of Scotland for Peterhead, coming twice within four days.

For both games we were in the hands Mr Bryan of Bryan's Coach and Van Hire of Denny, with an 8.15 a.m. departure scheduled from Firs Park. On the drive in from Edinburgh, a council truck was already plonking down the traffic cones outside Falkirk FC's stadium, a sure sign of a football club's affluence and expectation. I wondered whether at some stage in the dim and distant past they had ever coned-off the road to Firs Park. I doubted it.

Arriving for a later match, against Dumbarton, I thought the good times had indeed returned when I was met by a large tailback just outside the town. For the first time in living memory there appeared to be a queue of football traffic heading to the Shire. I was wrong. The hold-up was caused by a rogue cow, heavy with milk, trotting down the white line and peering into every car in the detached, incurious manner of cows everywhere. The Firs Park attendance that day was, in fact, 162.

The trip to Peterhead began badly for Ross Donaldson. He arrived yawning, unshaven and without a tie, and was immediately fined half a week's wages. This was all part of the manager's professional approach. The loss of a fiver will focus anyone's mind.

On the bus, I pondered where to sit. Should I be one of the boys or one of the staff? In the end I decided on the no man's land in between. The on-board entertainment choices were between, at the rear of the bus, the players' card school and, screening on video, *Ferris Bueller's Day Off.*

Quick wits, wheels and women – wish-fulfilment for footballers everywhere.

There was light-hearted banter behind and some earnest tactical discussions up front, but the mood changed dramatically after Dundee when the Fife sunshine gave way to an unnerving Aberdeenshire mist. Out of the gloom strange place-names emerged: Nether Finlarg, Muiryfaulds, Kirkbiddoo – this was alien territory. We felt akin to the Light Brigade wheeling into the wrong valley at Balaclava.

We had our own Raglan and Cardigan, too, Les Thomson and Alex Forsyth in isolated splendour in the tour guides' seats, much to the disgust of the manager who liked a crafty smoke down in the driver's well. The two directors exchanged not a word throughout the 300-mile round trip.

Balmoor, the new home of the Blue Toon, as Peterhead are mysteriously known, was a superb little arena. A salty sea breeze wafted in from the nearby coast and there was not a weed in sight on the green sward that was their pitch. The manager, mordantly, pointed this out to Jimmy Wilson.

With an hour to go before kick-off the Shire players were urged on to the pitch by Newall, where they huddled nervously in the centre circle, like penguins on a shore patrolled by killer whales. *San Francisco* was playing on the echoing tannoy, to the delight of Newall, plainly a child of the sixties. 'Aye, Scott McKenzie, great stuff,' he sighed dreamily.

'Is he playing for them?' asked an alarmed Kenny Quinn. 'I never saw him on their team sheet.'

'Aye, that's him sat up in the stand,' snorted the manager derisively.

A glance at the Peterhead team sheet confirmed the extent of their spending power: Shaun McSkimming, ex-Dundee, Robbie Raeside, formerly of Raith Rovers, and Jamie Buchan, son of Martin of Aberdeen and Manchester United fame. It was going to be a long, hard day.

Peterhead had only joined the Scottish Football League at the beginning of the 2000/1 season, having successfully fulfilled the wish-fantasies of the Shire board and sold their old ground, Recreation Park, to the supermarket chain Safeway. Their new home, and some new money, as so often, produced casualties.

Eighteen months previously I had sat alongside the then manager Ian Wilson at a Bell's Scottish Football League dinner. Like a nervous schoolboy, the former Scotland international had twitched and fidgeted in his chair before his award as Third Division manager of the season was announced. He was inordinately proud of what he had achieved in taking what was a small club to the brink of promotion. He revealed that he had been offered the chance to go to Inverness Caley Thistle but had turned them down because 'I have a great relationship with the chairman at Peterhead and didn't think the time was right'.

A season later, after a fifth place finish in Division Three, that chairman had fired him. The incestuous nature of Scottish football is best illustrated by the fact that Iain Stewart, the man Wilson had brought to the club as a striker, was promoted to replace him.

Newall had employed a friend to spy on the opposition the previous weekend and thus he was able to tick all the right boxes in his team talk. But, again, it was too quiet in the dressing room, the chemistry was all wrong. The Cat and his music apart, there was no emotion.

The manager spotted this, too, and tried a different theme, one familiar to any city dweller who has ever ventured into regions where there is more livestock than there are human beings: the southern states of America, West Cumbria, North

Wales . . . and the north-east of Scotland. We were in the land of *Deliverance* and *Duelling Banjos*, a land where the inhabitants have bad teeth and wear dungarees. Where, in the words of the comedian Bill Hicks, 'a man will offer to introduce you to his wife and sister – and they turn out to be the same person'.

'The shite opposition out there,' announced Dennis Newall, 'are all grouse beaters and sheep shaggers.' The city slickers would show these country bumpkins how it's done. The sheep shaggers and grouse beaters who made up the bulk of the Blue Toon support arrived in an advanced state of disorder after watching the Aberdeen v Rangers match on the social club's TV. 'You are in for a fucking humping,' one sneered at the Shire dugout.

And so it proved. Peterhead opened the scoring after eleven minutes with a diving header and on the half hour another accurate cross, and a mêlée in the Shire goalmouth, brought the second. At half-time, with the prospect of a heavy defeat looming, Newall launched into his charges with a tirade of frightening ferocity. Each player, his son, Chris, included, was lacerated in turn. He started at No. 1 and finished fourteen minutes later at No. 11. If the referee hadn't knocked on the locked door to call them out for the second half they would probably still be there, cowering on their benches in front of their irate manager.

I kept my eyes on the floor and thought back to our first meeting when Newall had agreed to have me in the dressing room – on two conditions: that I was not to quote him verbatim as 'my mum might read the book', and that I had to leave the dressing room if he really lost his rag. He made no such indication in those fourteen minutes. So this was him keeping his rag, then. God help us all.

The f-word and the c-word are the *lingua franca* of football

– Gordon Ramsay once played the game, after all – and I began to contemplate a book containing page after page of asterisks. Or a season spent in corridors outside a locked dressing room door. In the end, I compromised by taping his first team talk in a league fixture – at half-time in that away match at Peterhead – which I quote in full and his last, at full-time against the same team at Firs Park nine months later. Most of the ones in between were unforgettable, anyway. Readers of a delicate disposition should look away now.

'We shuffled about out there. You, you are looking at me as if I am wrong, Paul. I watch every second of every fucking game and you were ball-watching. See their playmaker, their number eight? How many times did he get fucking touches and spread it about? How many? And you won't accept that. See that acceptance, son? That's what will stop you getting to the next fucking level. Now, show us your quality, show us you're comfortable and start fucking closing down.

'Where's Chris Miller? You led those two shuffling about out there like two lambs to the fucking slaughter. See you, Chris, you are quite comfortable sitting out there and letting them breathe through their fucking arse. There's nothing's come out of you. Not a fucking thing.

'Gee, you're shelling balls in, there's no point if they're not there. You fucking tell them to come look for it. When we get the ball all of youse should be looking for it. There's no angles. You are fucking cheating on each other. You, Cat, you set the tempo of the game with that first fucking kick you took. How did we lose the second goal? You. We are playing like a bag of shite because of your kick-outs. Is that acceptable, Tony? (Nup.) I try fucking coaching you to kick the ball, to be comfortable. And you give us that. Come on, you are fucking killing us out there. Now let's get back to the fucking shape and discipline.

'Chris Miller, take the game up to them there. Get back to the fucking work-rate that's needed in the middle of that fucking park. We have played some nice fucking football, but there's no cutting edge. And the reason there is no cutting edge is that you don't have the fire in the belly you had last week. The game is still there for you. Tighten up in all departments. From now on we don't make fucking errors. And you fucking start working.

'You, Ross, gamble for the fucking thing. There's no point, Ross, just waiting for it to come to you. Fucking go looking for it. You have got to work your arse off. You are all working to some level, but I need you to step up the tempo. We are going to go out in the second half and give them a fucking run for their money.

'Changes. Chris, you go into the left-back position. Jamie, you go into right midfield. It will be a challenge for you, I know that, but you can mix it all you want in there. Don't switch off. Don't switch off and say, "Oh, fuck, this isn't going well for us". Fucking well get back to doing it. Drive it at the fuckers!'

A knock on the door, and a nervous-looking referee peering round it, brought the punishment to an end. Well, not quite. Next door, the Peterhead players were probably getting similar treatment from their manager – possibly something on the lines of 'if you can't do better than that against that shite next door then I'll find some who can' – and if anything they upped the tempo in the second half.

Buchan made the points safe with a twenty-yard shot low into the net after fifty-four minutes, before David Hagen ran unmolested through a petrified defence for the fourth. Ross Donaldson, being Ross Donaldson, was booked for unsporting behaviour before the Peterhead substitute – and throughout the season it was to be uncanny how replacements always managed to come off the bench to score immediately against the Shire – finished things off with virtually his first touch of the ball.

The full-time paint stripping was probably worse than at half-time, and on the way home the players remained traumatised in a state of total abjection, a sort of resigned shell-shock. The cards remained in their pack, the video screen remained blank.

Greig Denham was almost comatose in his misery, resisting all attempts by Dennis to engage him in conversation. He had plainly been used to better things. In an effort to cheer everyone up, Dennis produced a home video of a charity night at his old club, Albion Rovers, starring the worst stand-up comedian I have ever heard in my life. Not surprisingly, the Shire players did not exactly crack up at this.

Battered and bowed, we arrived back at Firs Park at ten past nine that evening, having spent thirteen hours of a summer Saturday on a journey to nowhere, the only material gain being the £10 (in coins), in a brown envelope, left on each seat. Or a fiver, in the case of the main striker. One by one, they filtered silently into the Falkirk night. 'Have a nice weekend, lads,' said the manager.

SHOWDOWN AT THE
STICKY CARPET

The seed corn of the British football game has always been the father and two sons, trotting out of the house at around two o'clock every Saturday afternoon; dad carrying a packed lunch and a flask, sons armed with scarves and a few pennies for a match programme. Love for the intangibility that is a football club is invariably handed down through the generations, often dating back to distant days when that club was founded.

That may have changed at the highest level, where surrogate fans – in recent times, notably those of Manchester United and Chelsea – have tended to attach themselves to success, or to what they see as glamour. At the level of the Scottish Third Division, the original justification for following a team home and away every weekend remains the same.

Scratch a Shire fan and you will probably find someone who grew up in Falkirk or who was transplanted there at an early age. He was probably introduced to the game by his father and has followed the team through thin and thinner ever since.

Some of the ones I met had been ball boys at Firs Park. Ian Ramsay, the chairman of the supporters' club, began to support them 'just to be different from my mates'. It goes without saying that the average Shire fan would have to pitch his expectations somewhat lower than, say, any other fan in the country. He would probably have learned that at an early age.

At one of their early matches, when the side were still embedded in a dreadful losing run, I was seated in the Firs Park stand when a ten year old, face almost invisible under a black and white scarf, turned to his father and asked: 'Dad, can I clap when we score?'

'Yes, son, but you'll be waiting a long time,' replied his father.

Four–nil down against Stenhousemuir at Ochil View, one Shire fan shouted from the terraces: 'Come on Shire, five–four will do.' Inured to the suffering that goes with being a Shire supporter, many of them have turned their side's haplessness into a positive. A mordant sense of humour comes with the territory; travelling to see their team lose every week has become like a medal of honour. Shorn of the need to be aggressive or rude about officials or opposition because their expectations are low to non-existent, the travelling Shire fans are probably the most popular in the league away from home.

A bad season for author and Arsenal fan Nick Hornby would be to see his team finishing second in the English Premiership; I have a hunch that most Shire fans would settle for that. To finish second bottom of the Scottish Third Division would probably spark dancing in the streets of Falkirk. But therein lies the dichotomy, because any measure of success would take away the whole *raison d'être* of the Shire – they would lose most of their eccentric worldwide support and they would certainly not have made the newspapers' sports pages as regularly. Not that this is how Newall and the players saw things. Whatever it might look like on the pitch, they were desperate to win.

During my season there, on away trips, some of the convolutions the fans subjected themselves to were mind-boggling in their complexity, although dictated by the fact that for obvious reasons none of them was prepared to drive. In the case of Elgin, for example, their dedication meant catching a 5.50 a.m. train from Falkirk, changes at Stirling and Aberdeen, arrival in Elgin at 10.56 a.m., return train from Elgin fifty-five minutes after the final whistle and eventual arrival back in Falkirk at 23.25 p.m. The previous season, for a trip to Peterhead, the trains from Falkirk were not running and a small group decided to take a taxi to Linlithgow, a train to Edinburgh, a train to Aberdeen and then a taxi, which cost them £55, to Peterhead. There they watched their side lose 6-0 before making the whole ghastly trek in reverse. Their devotion was almost mindless.

The hardcore of the Shire support is made up mainly of men in their mid-thirties to mid-forties, although two fans in their seventies – one infirm and supported by his friend – go to every match, home and away. And throughout the season I followed the team, mums and dads – notably those of the young strikers Derek Ure and Grant Findlay – saw virtually every fixture.

Home matches were invariably enlivened by four or five teenagers, quick-witted and sarcastic in the manner of Scottish youth, who always sat in the stand directly above the home dugout, a homemade Shire flag draped over the railing in front of them. I christened them the Dead End Kids and spent most matches praying that they wouldn't pick me as a target. They certainly picked on everyone else.

The Dead End Kids had a great line in patter and already possessed the sense of the absurd that goes with supporting the Shire. No one was safe. 'Pretend the ball's a pie,' they would chorus at Ross Donaldson. When another player shouted, in a moment of frustration, 'Fuck me!', one of them piped up without a moment's hesitation: 'Er, I'll pass on that one, Jimmy, thanks.'

They also had, for some unexplained reason, a passionate hatred of players with ginger hair – and there are a lot of them in Scottish football. Martin Bavidge of Peterhead, who did the Shire untold damage throughout the season, was a favourite target with a rising crescendo of 'Ginnnnngerrrr' greeting his every touch of the ball.

Their favourite player, possibly because he was not far off them in terms of age and looks, was Paul Ross, and Dennis Newall would be barracked unmercifully every time he brought the midfielder off. 'We want Paul Ross,' they would chant. 'Well, you can't have Paul Ross,' the manager would reply. Paul Ross himself would smile his fallen hero's smile of resignation.

Their humour could be wicked. Once, when The Cat went down at the feet of an opposing centre-forward and took a bad blow to the head, one of them called: 'Get the vet to put him down, he's still moving,' as the poor goalie writhed on the turf.

The vast majority of the support, however, belongs to the official supporters' club and I met some of this strange band early on in the season. They had requested the presence of Dennis Newall and Greig Denham at their Falkirk HQ, the Gordon Lounge – aka the Sticky Carpet – just round the corner from Firs Park on Thornhill Road. I got in by proxy.

The management had agreed to subject themselves to a question and answer session, although it promised to be confrontational. Dennis was still seething with anger after being told to 'Fuck off, Newall' by one fan as he left the field after the 6-0 defeat at Stenhousemuir in August. This supporter, quite understandably, found other things to do, but eleven others, a complete football team of ten males and one female, did show.

Their acknowledged leader was Ramsay, a forty-one-year-old production worker from Larbert, who acted as *de facto* chairman, and the remainder formed the bulk of the contributors to the acerbic and occasionally anarchic Shire Shout website. In many cases, football was the only reason for their friendship.

Dennis Newall, an avid reader of the posts on Shire Shout, worked through their names. 'Ramz' was obvious, as was 'Stewart, 36', a man in his mid-thirties called, eh, Stewart. 'Strumps' was also present, as were 'silentbutdeadly', 'mistereff' and 'wellibob'. 'Trevor the Terrorist' turned out to be a youth who looked about fourteen years old; 'dingotookmybaby', who posts some of the most damning comments from the safety of Australia, couldn't make it.

They had organised a table for the management team, and positioned themselves in a large semi-circle opposite. They seemed friendly enough, but the set-up gave every appearance of a court martial. There was a free drink from 'Ramz' for the three guests and a large plate of sandwiches. They had commandeered the snug, much to the disgust of one ancient regular deprived of his stool at the end of the bar. From time to time throughout the evening his face would appear in the glass of the swing door leading to the toilets, girning in anger and frustration, and lending a farcical edge to the proceedings.

Dennis introduced me and I gave a little speech about how the book would benefit the club and how I was looking forward to spending the season with them. One fan rose in the middle of my speech to go to the bar for another round of drinks but they did sit up and take notice when I mentioned that I had been granted access to the boardroom.

'But,' I told them, 'I am sworn to secrecy about what goes on there.'

'Don't worry,' said one. 'We know exactly what goes on there because the same thing has been going on there for twenty or thirty years.'

The questioning for the management team was hardly searching; it didn't tax either Denham or Newall. Why don't you play so-and-so? Why do you prefer Ross Gilpin to The Cat? Four-four-two, or four-five-one? That sort of thing.

Their questions about the prospects of the current team came suffused with a sort of resigned optimism. The manager had set an initial target of eight points by Christmas – the same total as the whole of the previous season. That caused a rustle of excitement in the Sticky Carpet, but the meeting almost dissolved into hysteria when he spoke of climbing off the bottom of Division Three for the first time in three seasons.

That feat would earn him the keys to Falkirk; they could start ordering the bubbly now. Their expectations, honed by years of disappointment, were almost laughable. One of them had been turned giddy with delight at the sight of Jamie Dunbar flicking the ball over an opponent's head and catching it on his instep. The fact that Dunbar had then passed the ball straight to the opposition mattered not a jot. Three passes strung together without the intervention of an opposing player was a major triumph. Hitting the woodwork was the stuff of dreams.

Time dragged on, and the pauses between questions grew longer, but they seemed unwilling to let us escape. Dennis and Greig were getting twitchy; I stole a sly look at my watch. Finally, the landlady marched in and started clearing the tables. The girning regular reclaimed his place at the bar. That appeared to be that, and we departed into a rainy Falkirk night.

'What did you think of that?' the manager asked me.

'Well, I'm sorry you have to go through things like that,' I replied.

Newall was indignant. 'No, you can't say that. This is part of being a manager. These people have paid their dues and you have to listen to what they have to say. I'm not going to agree with them, but you have to make the effort and listen. I wish the players had been there, it might have made them try a bit harder.'

The Shire players could be as perverse as their support. Having lost 5-0 at Peterhead in the opening league match, the CIS Cup tie four days later looked the safest of home bankers. Peterhead were plainly destined for better things and we also faced that draining 170-mile journey at a top speed of 55 m.p.h. Mr Bryan, even on motorways, stuck to that rigidly, mindful no doubt of his precious cargo.

The management's selection options had been narrowed by the fact that with a 2.30 p.m. start on a Wednesday from Firs Park a large chunk of the squad were unavailable because of work commitments. Ross Gilpin was in goal, with The Cat scowling on the bench. Newall had explained that with a general shortage of goalkeepers prepared to come and spend the rest of their careers picking a football out of a Shire net, he had to rotate the ones he had and endeavour to keep one, or both, from walking out and plying their trade elsewhere.

The cup tie was three minutes old when Martin Bavidge, the *bête rouge* of the Shire, let fly from thirty yards out and Gilpin's first touch of the ball was, of course, to pick it out of his own net. The goal provoked an outburst of unseemly gloating from a small army of local primary schoolchildren, still in their uniforms. 'Shire, you are shite, shite, you are Shire,' they chorused.

But at least this seemed to goad the sacrificial sheep. They certainly were not going to lie down for a shagging on this night. Paul Ross volleyed an equaliser and the Shire actually dominated for all of ten minutes. But they had used up all their good fortune. A linesman spotted an offence in the penalty box; Peterhead scored from the spot and a third goal put the tie beyond the Shire.

Substitute Gordon Parks scored a second but, as the commentators would say, it was too little, too late. A 3-2 defeat away at Peterhead, however, represented a moral victory for players and supporters alike and the five travelling fans – including striker Derek Ure's mum – went home happy. 'Two bloody away goals,' said one. 'I feel as if I've won the pools.'

'SHIRE HIT THE JACKPOT!' The newspaper headlines a week after the Peterhead match were announcing the unthinkable: the Shire, whose usual sponsorship came from the likes of Buildbase timber supplies, Rosebank Roofing and Les Mitchell, the Firs Park tannoy man, *had* won the pools.

Littlewoods, fighting a losing battle with the National Lottery, had just launched a £5m marketing campaign to woo back lost punters and, out of that, 'a six-figure sum' would be lavished on the worst team in Britain. The Shire board, struggling with a huge debt and facing the loss of £30,000 from the Pools Panel Promoters' Association, who had just pulled the plug on Scottish football, were suddenly the beneficiaries of the biggest windfall in their history.

The main question on everyone's lips was: Why? Why would Littlewoods choose to support Britain's worst football side? The answer was blindingly obvious: they couldn't get a foothold at a major club, so they did the next best thing and went to the other end of the UK's senior football pyramid. It was the sort of irony that the media loved.

In return for a few hoardings around the ground and the

Littlewoods – motto, Be Lucky – name on their shirts, the Shire would have their lives enriched. There would be a £50 win-bonus for players and for management, an exciting new website, a revamped programme and the opportunity to buy a Shire mousemat, Shire wallet, or a Shire mug via the online shop.

The website began in a megabyte of glory with some clever graphics and smart ideas, but soon lapsed into inactivity and was seldom updated. To fill out space, it relapsed into cliché. 'Several Things You Did Not Know About the Shire' was one topic. 'Did you know that . . . the chairman of East Stirlingshire FC is Alan J. Mackin?' it asked. And, of course, 'Did you know that Manchester United manager . . .' YES, I DID.

At other times, a contributor calling himself Littlewoods would announce with due graciousness: 'Thought all Shire fans would like to know that matchday admission to Saturday's game with Elgin City will be free. Littlewoods Pools are paying the normal admission cost on the fans' behalf, to allow the club to let everyone in for free.'

Littlewoods, in the tones of the posh announcer on the old Pathé newsreels would then add: 'Let as many people as possible know about it, so we can have a bumper crowd for what we hope will be the first win of the season.'

And, somewhat less graciously, 'For the sceptics among you, see Thursday's *Falkirk Herald* for details, and check the other Scottish papers over the next couple of days for news of the announcement. Those who come to the Elgin game will also get a voucher giving half-price admission to the following home game with Queen's Park. Littlewoods Pools will again be paying the difference.'

The pools people, by now at marketing warp speed, also announced the launch of their search for the Female Face of the Shire. A dodgy one this, as the notion of a wholesome young female Shire supporter prepared to wax lyrical about the virtues of family life, settling down and how much she wants to work with children and animals did not ring true.

Having stood impatiently many times in a lengthy queue at the Tesco newspaper kiosk in the central retail park, I can also safely say that the majority of the town's female population preferred the lottery to the pools.

But Brahm, the Littlewoods PR company, whose portfolio of clients includes Persimmon Homes, Chewits, Young's Seafood and Strathmore Water, pushed the boat out. There was a big launch day attended by most of the Scottish media and Les Thomson, Brahm and Littlewoods together fronted a press conference. Dennis said all the right things, and Greig Denham posed for pictures.

Littlewoods sat back to enjoy the publicity. If they had known that one of the Shire board hadn't wanted them within half a mile of his club, they might not have bothered. And that one director, to his eternal credit, remained cynical to the end. Pools companies or authors, they all came the same to him.

Writing in the Shire centenary booklet, in 1981, Alan McMillan had told the story of a board meeting in 1977, when a majority of directors wanted to make Billy Lamont the new manager. There was only one dissenter. Said to be 'fed up with Shire money being frittered away without consent', Alex Forsyth voted against. Suspicion and dissent seemed to have been written into his DNA.

He hadn't liked the idea of my writing a book (and he may have had a point there) and he certainly didn't like the idea of Littlewoods bailing the club out, particularly when they demanded reserved seating in the stand and somewhere to park their cars for free.

At one of the club's AGMs, at Grangemouth Town Hall, he had stormed out of the meeting following an outburst at Mackin. Forsyth had objected to the appointment of Douglas Morrison because the nomination 'had not been properly made at an earlier board meeting'. He went on to claim that the club was spending more than it was bringing in, adding: 'The board is trying to bankrupt the club so they can step in with a new rights issue and take over with one vote, one share. When Mackin came in he vilified the previous board for its financial performance, but he made it worse.'

Forsyth and his son-in-law, John Morton, had also been up in arms about the loan from McCabe and Mackin that had saved the club from bankruptcy, claiming that they had been excluded from that decision. All of which begged the question: Why stay on the board then? Morton supplied the answer: 'It's better fighting a fight inside the ring than being outside the ring.' And the old man had his boxing gloves on the night Littlewoods came to town.

We – I had been invited along on condition I stayed in a corner and looked like a piece of furniture – were attending the August board meeting. Mackin was away at his villa in Majorca, so vice-chairman Morrison was in charge of the proceedings. By now I had worked out the dynamics. The distance between Forsyth and his son-in-law from the rest of the board was not an accident at all; the two factions were obvious. Morrison may have held only a grand total of ten shares, but with Mackin and McCabe constituted a voting majority. Despite what they believed, Forsyth and Morton were the powerless dissenters.

The Littlewoods windfall was at the top of the agenda. It had been announced by their PR people as a six-figure sum, but the Shire board seemed to be discussing where

£10,000 would go, which, of course, is a five-figure sum – perhaps it would reach six figures if the team were to win their next seventy matches. It soon became clear, however, that their windfall was not going to go very far.

For a start, the club would have to pay back the £1,000 donated to them by their current shirt sponsor, McFaddens Timber, and there was a website to set up and bills from a printer of the new programmes. The emolument was vanishing fast.

But the marketing bling-bling and influx of fresh ideas from Littlewoods/Brahm seemed to be catching. The PR company also represented a company of landscape painters and Les Thomson had a brainwave: 'We should paint the grey concrete wall behind the goal at the Land of Leather end. Paint the heads of fans on it, like Arsenal did.' Even Alex Forsyth laughed at this one.

Brahm and the Littlewoods representatives were spending the night of the board meeting at the up-market Airth Castle Hotel just out of town and there was a half-hearted suggestion that all the directors should go and meet them. The problem was that, with the exception of Forsyth, who always wore tie, collar and suit, none of them was dressed for it.

Finally: 'Do we accept the last minutes?' asked Morrison. 'With reluctance,' said Forsyth with a pointed look in my direction. Then he started. He questioned the role of Littlewoods. They had asked for two reserved places in the car park – a car park which belonged to Comet – and four seats in the directors' box. 'Are they trying to take over the running of club?' he asked. Then, slowly and with great deliberation: 'I dinnae like the notion of Greeks bearing gifts.'

The meeting moved on and there was some desultory talk about the provisional sale of the stadium. It had gone for £1.3 million, £300,000 less than the original valuation.

'Will the shareholders see some benefit?' asked Forsyth. No-one seemed to know, or care, where they would go once it was sold.

Then it was on to the real business of the night. Enough of these six-figure sponsorship deals and potential uprooting of the whole club. John Morton cleared his throat and said: 'I have had a lot of complaints about the pie shop not being open at the last home game. Punters have been giving me hell about it and I don't blame them.'

'It's just not on,' agreed his father-in-law.

'Well, we should certainly try and do something about that,' said the man in the chair.

Apparently, there had been a bid from a rival pie and Bovril franchise which had caused a glitch in the Shire's bureaucratic processes. The dilemma was whether to stick with the tried and trusted or go into partnership with a new one who had promised extra onions with the burgers. And so it was agreed: Les Thomson would look into the matter and try and get the pie wagon up and running by the time Gretna arrived for the first home league match of the season. The consensus was to stick with the established vendor and to hell with the Greeks bearing extra toppings.

BIG TIME BILLYS

By the time the visitors' luxury bus pulled into the Land of Leather car park, the pie wagon was up and running. Housed in an identical Portakabin to the boardroom's, but on the other side of the main stand, it was staffed by a genial family of Scots–Indians. Their non-appearance the previous Saturday, however, had roused the wrath of the regular punters and they wanted redress.

One, obviously suffering from pie-withdrawal symptoms, got into a row with the owner about the lack of refreshment at the Berwick game. The owner, already counting the financial cost of a week's closure through no fault of his own, bridled at this and was all for stepping outside and settling the dispute in the time-honoured Scottish fashion of a 'square go' when a small, fat man in a dark suit stepped in. 'Any trouble, just let me know,' said the self-appointed mediator, drawing himself up to his full five foot six. 'I . . . am the general manager . . . of Gretna Football Club.'

'Get away, you're not,' said the incredulous punter.

'I certainly am.'

'Well, why don't you fuck off back to Gretna FC and take the rest of those fucking Fancy Dans with you.'

Gretna's fanciest Fancy Dan was David Bingham, who had enjoyed a fine career in the Scottish Premier League, notably with Dunfermline and Livingston. His previous club,

Inverness Caley Thistle – managed by his friend and Edinburgh neighbour John Robertson – had just won promotion to the top flight, but Bingham had jumped ship, dropped three divisions, and joined Gretna. Instead of Celtic Park or Ibrox, he was now playing at Ochilview, New Bayview and Firs Park. Many Scottish football folk wondered how one player's ambition could subside so quickly. The answer was simple.

A week earlier I had asked Robertson, who had moved on to manage Hearts, if he had considered signing Bingham to add experience to what was a very young Hearts side. 'Nah, I couldnae afford him now,' said Robertson.

Bingham, known as Bingo, was said to be on £1,500 a week and really was only playing the system. At thirty-three, he was close to the end of his career and had a young family and a four-wheel-drive vehicle to maintain. And he had company. Gretna were a full-time side who started the season with twenty-six players, many of them well-known names: Alan Main, the former Scotland goalkeeper, Derek Townsley, Stephen Cosgrove, Jamie McQuilken, Danny Lennon and Steve Tosh could all boast experience at the top level of the Scottish game. Their manager, Rowan Alexander, was unarguably the best paid outside the Scottish Premier League and probably better paid than most of them, and he had built one of the best squads in any league.

The funding had come from a Carlisle-based businessman called Brooks Mileson, who was said to be worth £46m. Mileson was the Roman Abramovich of provincial Scotland. He had promised eventually to build a 6,000-seat stadium in preparation for the day when Gretna would rise to the SPL, a towering ambition for a club whose average gate was less than 100 before Santa Claus arrived.

If they were top by Christmas, he vowed, they would

earn a sunshine break in La Manga. Not surprisingly, this produced a lot of envy everywhere. There was a discernible desire among other Third Division clubs to bring the Fancy Dans down a peg or two.

In the week before the match I asked Dennis Newall who was going to mark Bingham – who would 'pick him up', in the vernacular. He replied: 'Hopefully, the road sweeper on Firs Street come Monday morning.'

He carried a similar tactical plan into his team meeting. 'These are nothing but a team of Big Time Billys,' he said. 'They are on mega money and think they are someone. They are no-one. That Bingham, what's he doing playing here? Townsley, they're slumming it and they think you're just here to make up the numbers. Now, when they have the ball, you go right through them. I want their physio to be living on that pitch. Now are we up for this?' A few tentative nods and the odd 'Yuuus'.

'I can't hear you!'

'Yuuuuuuuus.'

The Cat put on *Eye of the Tiger* and went into his Rocky routine, the others high-fived each other, shook hands and slapped each other on the back. Then it was out to meet the Big Time Billys.

There was evidence everywhere of the Gretna affluence. Apart from a general manager who doubled up as a United Nations peacekeeper, a spy in the stand was seated with his curly-wurly earpiece and clipboard. Kenny Quinn, armed only with a pencil and his Oyez Straker shorthand notebook, looked on enviously.

Nearby, a stunning footballer's wife, resplendent in skintight white trousers and displaying a perfect bare midriff, tried in vain to cope with a three-year-old child. Occasionally, she would get up out of her seat and chase the errant boy down the walkway in front of us, with 100 eyes tracking her.

But, if Gretna had Brooks Mileson, we had Littlewoods. Some brand new signs shouting 'Be Lucky' were propped against the Land of Leather end and half-a-dozen men in business suits were in their reserved places in the box. Alex Forsyth, gibbering away to himself, sat alone.

Gretna were coming off the back of successive wins, 3-0 and 6-0, and were soon into a well-rehearsed routine with the strikers running off Bingham. His cross was headed in for the opening goal, but the Big Time Billys were not going to have it all their own way.

Shire full-back Chris Miller, after two free kicks that landed in the Land of Leather car park, summoned up a fantastic Beckham-esque effort for the equaliser. Newall was ecstatic about the possibilities of Miller in dead-ball situations after this, but the player then fell heavily in a tackle and was carried off. He wasn't to play again all season and one of the Shire's few attacking ploys had been strangled at source. The Curse of the Shire had struck again.

After Miller's momentous goal, the first as it was pointed out to us by the exultant voice on the tannoy against Gretna that season, the Shire switched off and a horrendous defensive error allowed Townsley to stab home the winner. Newall threw on his supersub, the effervescent Glaswegian Gordon Parks. And it almost worked. Parksy almost made his own headlines at once with a goal that was disallowed for offside and a shot against the cross bar in the last minute. Unfortunately, most of us missed this, as Footballer's Wife had chosen that moment to leave the stand, hand in hand with child and white pants stretched taut. 'Mommy, mommy, is daddy a winner?' cried the child. It was agreed by all that daddy was, indeed, a winner.

The Stirlingshire Cup may not quite have the same resonance as, say, the Champions League, but the competition, run on a round robin basis, was a useful little earner for the Shire. And they had won it twice.

On a balmy evening in August, Dumbarton FC arrived for the first round proper. This, however, raised the question: What were the Sons of the Rocks, whose home is some sixty miles away, doing in the Stirlingshire Cup? No-one seemed able to supply an answer, so I simply assumed that it was like Wimbledon or the World Cup and open to all-comers.

The Shire's tannoy announcer Les Mitchell (it often baffled me how he kept his job) began the proceedings by making a laboured head count of the directors present. 'Two of them,' he said. 'Nice of you to join us, gentlemen.' Mitchell also demanded support for 'the only club in the centre of Falkirk', which may sound pedantic, but strictly speaking was true. He had hardly got the words out, however, before he was busy naming opposition goal-scorers.

The Shire began brightly, but then lost a goal from a breakaway and subsided into incompetence. With passes finding only the opposition and the defence losing all shape, Dumbarton scored two more.

But there were some positives. The Cat saved a penalty and was named man of the match, occasioning a rare smile. The previous week, Ross Gilpin had been man of the match, so while being a keeper at the Shire had its downsides, not least being the most overworked man on the park, there was the odd bonus, like a bottle of Bell's Whisky or a drinks' voucher for the Gordon Lounge.

Football rivalry is a strange thing, particularly in Scotland. Celtic and Rangers can justify some historical enmity, but some of the other rivalries, derby matches as they are known, are hard to fathom. St Johnstone, who are based in Perth, loathe Dundee, who are not even geographically close. There are three senior sides in Angus, but only Arbroath and Brechin count as a local derby; Montrose don't get a look in. In the south of Scotland, Stanraer v Queen of the South is the ritual annual bloodletting and the clubs are eighty miles apart.

In the absence of Falkirk, who had moved on to higher things, the match against Stenhousemuir had become the local derby for the Shire. The Mighty Warriors, as they are known, prefer to look on Stirling Albion as the team that must be beaten at all costs, but Stirling Albion, too, had escaped to a higher division. The Shire were the next best thing. Being local, of course, meant that we all travelled to Ochilview under our own steam. Parking was in the main street outside the stadium. The residents clearly objected: there was much aggressive moving of curtains when I arrived.

Stenhousemuir, uniquely for a Scottish Third Division side, don't have an overdraft, possibly because they never spend any money on the ground. This information came from an elderly gateman, who told me he had followed the Warriors for fifty-four years and had never missed a home match 'except when the wife was ailing and I had to take her to hospital when I should have been coming to the match. I still made it for the second half, though.'

'And what happened to your wife?'

'Oh, she died a week later.'

His side, he said, had spent a season sharing with Falkirk until Westfield Stadium was ready, but the temporary stands needed to cater for First Division crowds had been removed and the ground was now 'back to normal, which is nice'.

'You see the police station in the corner?' he asked, pointing to an ancient Portakabin with a faded sign outside saying 'Police'. 'That's from the days when we used to have crowds here. They've all gone now, of course. Three men and a dog could control the crowds here now.'

It was a glorious late summer day, without a cloud in sight, and I happily took in the distant prospect of the Ochil Hills. 'Well, at least the view has never changed,' I said. 'Do you know what they say about the Ochils?' asked the gateman. Well, I could hazard a guess, as I had heard the same hoary legend about distant landmarks about a thousand times. I had heard this rural wisdom in various languages about Mount Cook, Mont Blanc, the Tre Cime de Lavaredo, Ben Nevis, Snowdon and Pendle Hill.

'No, what do they say about the Ochils?'

'When you can see the Ochils it's about to rain and when you can't see them it is raining,' he said. 'Do you want to buy a programme?'

Four games into the season, and I still wasn't feeling like a piece of furniture. I didn't like catching players' eyes when Newall tore into them, quite often feeling I was intruding into private grief. The £1 invested in the Warrior programme (main sponsor: Professional Office Supplies) did give the opportunity to keep my head down in my studies as the manager appealed to their character, their heart, their spirit.

Like every other programme at every other club, the manager's musings in the Stenhousemuir version contained dire warnings about the penalties of not giving the Shire due respect. 'We will need to play to our full potential if we are to take anything from this game,' wrote Des McKeown in his Boss Talk column.

They certainly did that. With their strings tugged by one of Newall's 'flash gits in fancy boots' – a former Motherwell team-mate of Greig Denham's called Paul McGrillen – they overran the Shire to the tune of 6–0. Striker Joe Savage helped himself to a hat-trick and Newall went nuclear. 'It's clear some who are here will be going as they are not good enough,' he warned. I looked up from the page carrying the list of Warrior Goldline winners to find most of his players eyeing each other and wondering who he meant.

Outside, a fine rain had begun to fall. The gateman smiled a 'told you so' and I was passed at high speed by Savage, a Stenhousemuir official in hot pursuit. 'Joe,' he pleaded. 'You cannae leave with the match ball. We dinna have enough of them.'

I arrived back at the car to find a printed note stuck on the windscreen. 'No Football Parking Here,' it read. And, in smaller letters: 'At Your Peril.'

A friend had told me a rather poor joke about the town of Cowdenbeath in the week before the Shire's first visit of the season. 'I went in a pub and found Kate Adie and Martin Bell serving behind the bar,' he had said. Tasteless it may have been, but he may have had a point. It's a one-street town with the ubiquitous leisure centre fighting a losing battle with rough-looking pubs and fast-food joints. It is one of only two towns in Britain where nurses can buy a home with a traditional mortgage of three times their salary.

Central Park, the home of the football club, also doubles as a stock car stadium and is a place where, apparently, tractors go to die. A huge compound close to the entrance houses some of the rusting wrecks. The ground barrier between crowd and pitch consists of a scatter of enormous tyres, along with an eight-foot-high fence. This, I was informed, is not to keep fans out, à la Serie A in Italy, but to prevent wheels from careering into the stand and decapitating the watching support.

That said, Cowdenbeath are, it seems, a well-run club,

without debt and with an excellent youth system. The financial security is based on the stock car racing income and the board's refusal to live above its means. All that may be true, but I can still offer one piece of advice to them which would increase revenue no end: invest in a decent-sized wall around the ground. I arrived to see several heads peering over a three-foot-high perimeter.

Cowdenbeath, presumably in a longing deference to Pele et al., rejoice in the title of the Blue Brasil. They are one of several clubs locked in the lower reaches of Fife but, as they like to point out, they are the oldest senior football club in the kingdom. They have seen better days, mainly in the 1930s, when several thousand fans would flock to Central Park.

Like the Shire, their history is speckled by setback. In the 1939/40 season they were fined what was then a colossal sum of £5,000 for not fulfilling a fixture. The excuse that several key players had enlisted in HM Forces cut no ice with the league committee. Cowdenbeath responded by resigning, were not readmitted until long after the war and it had been all downhill from there.

For the next quarter of a century Cowdenbeath languished in the Second Division, but they could boast the statutory near miss against one of the Old Firm: a 3-2 League Cup first-leg win against Rangers at Ibrox in 1949. The second leg attracted a record crowd of 25,000 to Central Park to see Rangers win 5-4 on aggregate after extra time.

Since then, the Blue Brasil had enjoyed more downs than ups. After a gap of twenty-two years, they won promotion again in 1992, followed by an embarrassing run of thirty-eight league matches without a home win. With the club entrenched at the bottom of the league and crowds dwindling away to a mere handful of diehards, the footballing future looked bleak.

Things began to turn around with the arrival of Craig Levein, later to win fame at Hearts and Leicester. A former player, he took the club close to promotion but then did a Fergie and left mid-season to join Hearts.

This was to be Greig Denham's comeback match after battling his long-term knee injury. He had trained assiduously on those wonky knees but admitted he was far from fit. He looked distinctly ill at ease: 'I'm more nervous today than going to Celtic Park or Ibrox,' he said. 'But at least you'll get a rest from me effing and blinding in the dugout.' He need not have worried. Kenny Quinn, promoted to pitchside from his usual place in the stand, turned out to be blessed with the same gift.

Greig, true to the tactical plan demanded by his manager that 'we should get stuck into these fuckers from the start', made his mark at once with a scything tackle that sent the opposing centre-forward up into the air. He noticeably ran out of steam after that. But the club's new signing, Joe Robertson – a lantern-jawed Glaswegian built like a lightweight boxer – at least gave them the lead, scoring with his first touch of the ball in Shire colours. 'Blow the whistle now, ref,' demanded Dennis Newall.

Everything was going right. Ross Donaldson hit the bar. The travelling Shire fans began a disjointed chant of 'Shire-ione', as in 'Champ-ione' and for the first time in living memory some of them moved optimistically at half-time to stand behind the opposition goal for the second half.

I forsook the delights of the half-time team talk for the delights of the Blue Brasil boardroom. I was impressed. This was a club which did things in style. There was a steaming buffet, silver service and all the directors wore suits. The reason for such pomp became clear, however, when the boardroom door opened and a distinguished, silver-haired gentleman with a military moustache, accompanied by an equally distinguished lady in a floral dress walked in: Lord and Lady MacFarlane of Bearsden KT, the nearest thing Scottish sport has to royalty, were exercising their *droit de seigneur*.

Lord Mac's Bell's Whisky company sponsorship had kept most Scottish league clubs outside the SPL alive and he is a football nut, well, an aristocratic football nut. He had played for Queen's Park and is the club's honorary patron. His involvement in football is such that he claims to visit every football ground outside the SPL, along with Lady Mac, every season and offers a gallon bottle of Bell's whisky for the club that serves the best pies.

Lord Mac is quite finicky about his pies: 'They have to be heated to the proper temperature and nicely presented. It's often about the crispness of the outer crust.' Needless to say, this is another trophy that the Shire have never won.

The match, which ended in a 2-1 win for the Blue Brasil, had been hard-fought and, as Dennis Newall said later, his team had not enjoyed the bounce of the ball. The home side's second goal had taken a wicked deflection. But, as the manager observed – and he seemed to have a never-ending and instantaneous supply of such information – the Shire now hadn't earned an away point, let alone a win, since January 2003. They did not, in other words, travel well.

He was not best pleased. The main question for everyone in the dressing room after the match was whether Newall, having criticised everyone else, would give his pal Greig a similar bollocking. Greig did it for him, admitting that he was unfit and accepting responsibility for the winning goal.

Five minutes before the final whistle a fantastic cacophony from the car park had drowned out the effing and blinding on the pitch. It had sounded like the arrival of a Panzer

Division. I walked out to find the car park clogged with strange machines manned by even stranger drivers. The real business of the day was about to get under way. 'Have youse fuckers finished with our park?' demanded a middle-aged man dressed in red and black leathers and carrying a crash helmet.

In early September we lost our first member of the backroom team. Newall and Denham had decided that physio Laura Gillogley was, in their words, 'a disruptive influence'. A new management team invariably want their own back-up, but the seeds for this had been sown at a confrontational meeting early on in the season.

Laura, Jimmy Wilson, Dennis and Greig were there. Les Thomson took the chair. Jimmy took umbrage about some mild criticism of the state of the pitch. Les ordered Dennis only to wear tracksuits adorned with the Buildbase logo and decreed – much to Dennis's disgust – that there would be no more smoking on the bus. Laura's days were numbered when she complained about being spoken to like a sixteen year old. 'Youse two are the worst I have ever worked with,' she told Newall and Denham. They insisted she had lost the confidence of the players.

It was left to chairman Mackin to ring her later and do the deed, whereupon Laura announced that she was going to take them to an industrial tribunal. Like many former Shire employees, Laura was to go on to better things, landing a job with the SPL side Livingston.

Early in September, the Shire's fall guys arrived after the long trek from Elgin, the most distant fixture on the map. Or at least some of them did. Like the Shire, they have few indigenous players and most of their squad was drawn from the Central Belt, and, like the Shire, most of them make their own way to away games. At least they try to.

Sure enough, three of them, travelling together, turned up at the ground in Falkirk at half past one, kit in hand and raring to go. A deserted ground they probably expected; a locked ground they probably didn't. Undeterred, they asked a kindly pensioner when the Shire crowds usually began to appear.

'Oh, around one-ish, to soak up the atmosphere.'

'So where are they?'

'Where they always are for home games – at Firs Park. This is Falkirk's stadium.'

A mad dash across the town's noisome one-way system brought the three lost souls to Firs Park, flushed with embarrassment, with minutes to spare.

The Shire had six frontline players missing through injury, including new man Joe Robertson and winger Chris Baldwin (laid low by an in-growing toenail); Chris Newall was forced to take to the field with damaged ribs and, still waiting for his work permit, Shaggy had yet to play a game. The 1-0 win to the visitors did not come as much of a surprise.

I arrived to find the chairman in the dressing room. Earlier in the week one of the player's irate fathers had telephoned Newall to order him to 'go easy on the lads', now he was there to check up in person. While Newall gave his team talk, language and manner carefully modified, Mackin, trying not to look as though he was eavesdropping, visited the adjoining toilets where he took the longest piss on record. When he finally appeared round the corner, ostentatiously buttoning up his flies, Newall had to introduce him. Until then, some of the players believed I was the chairman. 'This is the chairman,' said Newall. 'He is going to say a few words.'

Mackin's speech was short and sweet and couched in

the language of the old pro: 'Youse lot. Youse lot are lucky bastards still to be playing,' he said bitterly.

By now I had realised that when whoever watches over Scottish football came to bestow their largesse, East Stirlingshire FC were last in the queue. The facilities, the finance, the playing staff and much on the periphery were at the lower reaches of the sporting food chain. The Shire had been left with the residue of almost everything.

On match days, Firs Park was patrolled by half a dozen stewards who, on the face of it, would be hard pressed to control an outbreak of unruliness in a crèche and the first-aiders looked as if they had been recruited from a local old folks' home. Their working day at Firs was almost a sinecure.

No-one on the terraces, to my certain knowledge, has suffered a heart attack brought about by the excitement on the field and the level of commitment there, in the case of the Shire players at any rate, made anything more than the occasional bruise – easily dealt with by a physio – remote. Crowd violence at Firs was an unlikely concept, too. The numbers of visiting fans seldom rise above double figures and the local support were long ago sedated into something approaching narcolepsy.

Ground control while I was there was in the hands of the most unlikely band of enforcers, including a girl of six-teen who went about her business in a curiously juxtaposed combination of cutaway top and furry boots. She may have been the bonniest match-day steward in Britain, but most Saturdays was hard-pressed to control the Dead End Kids in the main stand who, in the manner of teenagers everywhere, were loath to take orders from a 'burd' not much older than them. Most of the time she had to phone in the reinforce-ments to quell outbursts of insubordination.

Another, older, girl seemed traumatised by her responsibilities. Both were supplied by Care in the Community. The two other stewards were male, but aged and with the broken-veined, red-nosed complexions of retired racehorse trainers. Their pre-match preparation consisted of the swilling of several large mugs of sweetened tea in the players' kitchen. But if push ever came to shove and soccer hooliganism did show its ugly head at Firs Park, the club could always fall back on the Terrible Twins, Mark and Mal, the twenty-stone guardians of Shire law and order.

Mark was the head steward, the coordinator. When I first arrived at the Shire he had slipped easily into Jobsworth mode, questioning my credentials, my birthright and, above all, my qualifications for using the players'/directors' entrance, that precarious flight of aluminium steps leading down to the flagged path skirting the boardroom.

For a whole season Mark remained unmoved by my press pass, computer case and the plea that 'I'm with the Shire'. At every home game I would be welcomed with the same look of undisguised hostility and the question: 'Can I help you, mate?'

Once, when Mark had plainly got out of bed on the wrong side that morning, I had to ring Les Thomson in his office and plead for admittance. And all the while a stream of freeloading fans sneaked past behind us, unchallenged.

For the sake of a change of scenery and a different perspective, I went to sit on the condemned terrace after the interval of the Elgin game, planting myself a few yards from two schoolboys dressed in Shire colours. I had just made myself comfortable when Mark, cup of tea in one hand and two pies in the other, hustled over to tell me to move.

'Youse cannae sit here,' he told me.

'But those kids are sitting here.'

'They don't count. You'll have to go in the stand.'

'Well, if they can sit here, why can't I? I'm writing a book about the Shire.'

'Well, you can write your book about the Shire somewhere else. And anyway, that one there,' pointing to a boy with glasses, 'is Derek Ure's brother. He can sit wherever he wants.'

For the first time I noticed that the security at Firs didn't run to walkie-talkies and curly-wurly earpieces . . . they communicated by mobile phone. Mark had a tattoo across four large knuckles: S C O T.

The security at most grounds throughout the season, Firs Park excepted, usually succumbed to the magic password: 'I'm with the Shire'. Even at Falkirk, who were priming themselves for the SPL, it was a simple matter to get past the black-suited bouncers outside the doors marked players and directors only. 'I'm with the Shire.'

'OK, mate, on you go. Away dressing room first on the right down the corridor.'

At the time of the Shire's second, and final, match in the round robin Stirlingshire Cup, and the meeting with their traditional rivals, Westfield Stadium was only half completed, with a huge cantilever stand, capacity 4,200, housing all fans. Three large tracts of space yawned on either side. The facilities inside were impressive, with lavish changing and hospitality areas and showers the size of a small ballroom. The dugouts were larger than the Shire home dressing room.

Falkirk had the technology to match. Sitting in the away dressing room a blue light, accompanied by a wailing siren, suddenly started flashing in the corner. We all looked at each other wondering where the fire assembly point was and trying, as you do when a fire alarm sounds, to work out what personal possessions we could escape with.

As we barged past each other to get through the door, it

suddenly dawned on us when we saw no-one else in the corridor – it was the five-minute warning before kick-off. We shuffled back inside. Whereupon the referee, plainly just as immune to high technology, knocked on the door and began to shoo the players out on to the pitch. 'Come on, Shire. Fucking last again,' he guffawed.

We had arrived early on a Tuesday night in September and eagerly examined the opposition team line. As expected, Falkirk had shown scant respect and had decided to field a team of youngsters reinforced only by a couple of regular first-teamers. Portuguese striker Pedro Moutinho was up front, but they had a sixteen-year-old at full-back. One name, however, stood out. The Falkirk No. 5 was listed as J. Hughes (capt). 'Oh fuck,' said one of the Shire strikers.

John 'Yogi' Hughes was one of the best-known characters in Scottish football. Named after another Yogi Hughes, a Celtic player from the sixties distinguished as much by being part of the Lisbon Lions squad when they won the European Cup in 1967 as for his off-field antics, the Falkirk player-manager had forged a distinguished career with Hibs, Celtic and Ayr United.

He had taken over as Falkirk player-manager in 2003 and, as at every other club, had swiftly become a cult hero. Even Yogi – and everyone, including his wife, calls him Yogi – would admit that his career wasn't built on subtlety, rather on a whole-hearted commitment and physical intimidation.

In an interview I did with him for a Bell's-sponsored football book in 2003, it also became clear that here was the original poacher turned gamekeeper. Most of his fund of stories was heavily censored by Bell's, who seemed particularly alarmed at any mention of drink-fuelled escapades in their book; odd coming from Scotland's biggest purveyor of blended whisky to the nation.

At the time of the Stirlingshire Cup match, Hughes was two days away from his fortieth birthday and obviously thought that some sort of gesture was appropriate, some sort of two-fingered gesture at that. He decided to have a run-out against the Shire.

As a lesson in controlled intimidation, the ninety minutes Hughes spent on the field were awe-inspiring. Gordon Parks, making his first start of the season in place of Ross Donaldson (and I would have paid good money to see Hughes take on him) got an elbow in his Adam's apple at his first touch. Jamie Dunbar had his ankles taken away from behind. The referee turned a blind eye to both incidents.

After that, there were few problems with the Shire attack and Hughes could show off a bit, aiming long balls out of deep and occasionally bursting into the needless sprints of a man proud of his fitness. Falkirk won 5-0, Hughes left the field to rapturous applause, and the Shire players retired to count their bruises.

Methil, the battered Fife town that is the home of East Fife FC, also sees a lot of blue flashing lights, usually on a Friday and a Saturday night. One of the most deprived areas in Scotland after the coal pits that once supplied most of the work to the town's labour force went belly up, the High Street is a maze of cut-price supermarkets and shops offering to cash DHSS cheques. Even some of the pubs in the area are boarded up: a certain sign of terminal decay.

The town had once thrived on its status as Scotland's largest coal port with an indigenous population housed in attractive sandstone tenements. But in the seventies the area had been almost completely razed. Modern council housing sprung up where the tenements once stood. The housing schemes brought the inevitable overspill from Glasgow. East Fife, the football club, was once an integral part of the community; now most of the town's football-supporting youth head for Ibrox or Celtic Park on a Saturday lunchtime.

But whoever runs the club, they are good housekeepers and, in Scottish Third Division terms, fairly progressive. They have a woman director on the board and are one of the few clubs in Scotland to boast a second-year-in-a-row profit. They spent that profit, some £77,000, on buying their New Bayview stadium – they had moved from Old Bayview in 1998 – and its associated land.

The East Fife board runs a tight ship and had recently turned down repeated requests from fans to have Sky TV installed in the supporters' lounge; the board did their homework, worked out that a twelve-month subscription to Sky would be £2,400 plus a larger screen TV and decided to stick with Grandstand. The money they would have spent went into manager Jim Moffat's transfer budget instead.

New Bayview is close by the shore, with a fierce sea breeze from the Firth of Forth wafting along the romantically titled Harbour View on which the ground stands. But there is little other romance about the surroundings. A massive, redundant power station looms on one side and most of the ground is open to the elements.

As always, there was a friendly home fan to fill me in: Methil Power Station had once run on the washings from coal mines. But the mines were no more. Since 2000, the building had been maintained as part of a strategic reserve by Scottish Power. 'Do you know what they say round here about Methil Power station?' he asked. 'Yes, I do,' I said, hurrying inside.

The Shire's new physio, David Jenkins, or DJ as he likes to be called, was making his debut. He was all brisk efficiency, talking to players like a benign doctor talking to his patients and in a strange language of plantars, cruciates, hip flexors and adductors. He works part-time at Glen Ochil prison just outside Falkirk and also possesses a refereeing qualification.

He told me about the ancient art of pre-match rubdowns. Only one player in the Shire team, apparently, asked for massage before a game.

'Lucky for you,' I said.

'Why's that?'

'Well, if you had to rub down all eleven of them you'd be knackered. Why don't you get them to shave their legs, like professional cyclists?'

DJ began to edge slowly away from me. He suddenly found other things to do.

The dugouts were on the far side of the pitch, in the shadow of the power station where, in the absence of any meaningful action on the field, most of the entertainment came from the body language of the respective managers. They live every minute of the game, prowling up around the so-called technical area in front of the dugouts, talking to the skies, appealing to no-one in particular and asking rhetorical questions of themselves: 'Why can't I find a striker who can hold the ball up?' 'See that bastard? He's killing us.'

Moffatt, a former goalkeeper, had 'been around', as they say, with spells at Manchester City, Montrose, Hamilton Accies, Dunfermline, Forfar Athletic, Brechin City, East Fife, Cowdenbeath, East Stirling and Albion Rovers. He has a foghorn voice and, rather than pithy statements, offers long, Agincourt-like speeches to his troops from the touchline. 'Hey, Fairy,' he'd yell. 'Why don't you take a gamble, move into the box when the keeper takes a by-kick and try and get a second ball. That way we might get something out of this fucking game.'

His assistant was a player called Kevin Bain and he knew all the tricks of an old pro. With the match goalless, he booted a ball that was heading out of play for an East Fife throw-in back to a home player; with East Fife 1-0 up, he let the ball run under his feet for a ball boy to chase.

These small boys, remarkably efficient and agile for the most part, slowed down noticeably once East Fife took the lead, one of them spending close to a minute to climb over a wall he had earlier vaulted in a trice.

Since East Fife's onfield strategy was built almost exclusively on a long-ball game, it was pretty stodgy fare, and the referee didn't help. John Robotham, the official who took charge of the 2005 Scottish Cup final, began his career as a linesman – at an East Fife v Albion Rovers game. The man with the flag on the other side of the park that day was Hugh Dallas, later to become a FIFA referee. You have to start somewhere, but the official at New Bayview was going nowhere.

A roly-poly little figure, at one point Dallas stood belly to belly with Ross Donaldson, like Tweedledum and Tweedledee discussing rattles and battles. Dennis Newall spent much of the match haranguing him and the linesman. At one point he even accused him of cheating.

The well-known referee Willie Young once told me that it was quite often a harder job being a linesman than a referee and I could see his point. A referee can quarter the pitch; a linesman has to keep up with players who are a lot younger and a lot quicker. And it must be awfully hard sprinting down a touchline with a flag clamped firmly by the knee. Newall has little sympathy: 'They're paid about £100 a week more than us,' he points out. 'They could at least get a few decisions right.'

At half-time, while the Young Fifers had their penalty

shoot-out, a female announcer – a very PC club East Fife – relayed the half-time scores, which are piped down into the away dressing room. 'East Fife one, East Stirlingshire nil,' she proclaimed to the sound of a weak cheer outside. And that is how it ended.

The half-time pie, tough and gritty as a lump of Methil coal, proved to be hard work and I had to break into a trot across the pitch to get back to the dugout in time. The players were already lined up in the centre circle. 'Why don't you walk through the Shire back four?' came a voice from the visiting fans' end. 'They won't notice you.'

Firs Park was beginning to get a bit crowded. The intruders – for that is how I looked upon them – were from *Front*, 'the sexiest, edgiest, funniest male lifestyle magazine in the UK packed with babes, sport, music, fashion, and loads, loads more'. The reporter was a shifty-looking character with bleached blond hair, the photographer a fat man who called the Shire players 'lads'.

I felt an irrational resentment at their arrival; they were on my territory. What is more, the reporter commandeered my place in the shower and I had to revert to the spot by the washing machine. We eyed each other with undisguised hostility across the dressing room floor.

They were here to spend a day – and a night as it turned out, since they followed the team to a local pub for drinks afterwards – with Britain's worst football team and their visit must have lived up to their expectations.

And the Shire were big news. *Front* apart, Ross Gilpin had been on Radio Scotland the night before to be interrogated about what it was like to spend a career picking the ball out of his net.

Queen's Park had upset the Gretna applecart the previous month when they beat the promotion favourites 3-2 and they were on a bit of a roll. They certainly rolled all over the Shire, winning 5-0. Ross Donaldson was taken off long before the end and poor David Harvey, the Shire's angelic-looking full-back, scored two own goals. Still, on the upside, he was now the club's top scorer that season.

There was also a rising wave of discontent sweeping the home terraces. Mackin was in the directors' box and most of it was aimed at him. 'Mackin, you are turning me into an alcoholic,' came one plaintive voice.

Littlewoods had decided, as part of their Shire charm offensive, that they would offer a man of the match prize. So now we had a Bell's man of the match, a Gordon Lounge man of the match and a Littlewoods man of the match. The Shire players were more decorated than Paolo Maldini.

Seated amid the detritus of discarded socks, boots, shin pads and water bottles in the dressing room later, poor David Harvey looked like a little boy whose pet puppy had just been put down. Dennis was remarkably restrained – possibly because of the presence of the *Front* man. He moved his counters over the magnetic board in an effort to show them where they went wrong, but no one looked interested.

Outside, the Shire's oldest living fan asked me if I would be going to the Albion Rovers match at Coatbridge the following weekend. 'If you are, and you want to use the shit-house, take your wellies,' he warned. *Front* magazine, as I had forecast to Dennis Newall, duly took the piss when it appeared a month later.

Cliftonhill, the home of Albion Rovers, was indeed an eye-opener. The ground is next door to the district magistrates' court and opposite a distillery. Football, 'beaks' and cheap blends; the abstracts of Saturdays in Coatbridge neatly compressed into a few hundred square yards.

Cliftonhill could have been the new Hampden, according to some. A vast tract of surrounding acreage was once owned by the club, but the previous chairman, a scrap metal merchant, gradually sold off the surrounding land to shabby housing schemes until all that was left was the derelict square known as Cliftonhill. The forsakenness of the whole place is best summed up by the main sponsors' advertising hoarding on the empty covered area opposite the main stand: Reigart Demolition.

The away dressing room was the size of a small broom cupboard, and devoid of coat hooks; the Shire players had to park their match suits on the wooden benches. In the corner, guarded by an open door hanging off its hinges, stood a single, filthy toilet. There was no paper, although, thoughtfully, an old copy of the *Coatbridge News* had been supplied.

Albion Rovers fans brought up amid this squalor are not noted for their subtlety. The level of abuse had to be heard to be believed, with most of it directed at a five-foot-tall referee. Many of the home fans were already drunk; one woman in her sixties, eyes glazed and almost incoherent, attempted to engage me in conversation: 'You see youse,' she said. 'Youse are in for a fucking humping.' Then at the referee: 'You are a wee shite.' She added, mysteriously: 'I know you.'

By way of contrast, when the official booked the equally diminutive Shire full-back David Harvey, a voice from within the tiny knot of visiting supporters told him: 'Pick on someone your own size, ref!'

Dennis Newall was plainly running out of motivational tools for his team talks. He had tried regional racism (sheep shaggers and grouse beaters at Peterhead) and inverse snobbery (Big Time Billys for Gretna) and he had appealed to his team's pride and spirit and greed (think of the £50 win bonus). This time, he demanded that they win this match on his behalf.

Newall had spent several years at Cliftonhill, as commercial manager and on the coaching staff, but when he went back in midweek to scout their game against Hibs in the CIS Cup they had failed to offer him a cup of tea. 'So let's go and fuck them for that,' he growled, slapping his palm on his inner elbow in the continental equivalent of the V-sign. The players looked unimpressed; in the background Joe Robertson could be heard hawking and spitting into the single filthy toilet bowl.

The Rovers' changing areas were down in the basement and this must be the only ground in Scotland where you have to climb a flight of stairs, past a couple of bars oozing rank beer and cigarettes, before reaching daylight, the pitch and a volley of abuse – much of it aimed at Dennis Newall – from the terraces above. The air of unreality – or maybe the air of wishing that I was elsewhere – was reinforced by the sight of an enormous fat man ambling out behind us, dressed in the home strip. I thought he was some punter from a local pub who had won the Wee Rovers draw and was being rewarded by the opportunity to warm up with the first team on a match day. But, amazingly, when the referee blew to start the match, he remained on the pitch. What is more, the expected derision from the terraces did not emerge. He was obviously a fixture there.

Mark Yardley was his name and he made Ross Donaldson look dainty, but after a time I began to feel that there was something heartening in the sight of a man who looked like Hattie Jacques playing football, and playing in Coatbridge what is more, where, as I have mentioned, the fans are not renowned for their subtlety. It reinforced the old adage that it is a game for all shapes and sizes. Yardley's idea of work-rate consisted of walking from the halfway line into the Shire penalty box and back again. His party piece was to trap the ball on his stomach.

We had media royalty in the stand: Jim Traynor, who lives just down the road in Airdrie, was there to comment on proceedings for the *Daily Record*. Traynor, known in Scotland for his trenchant views on the game, as well as a phone-in during which he takes great delight in cutting off outraged punters in full flow, had plenty to write about. Most of it was about Yardley, but the 3-3 draw, with all the goals in the first half, offered him additional material – and to his eternal credit, he resisted the temptation to patronise. It was the Shire's first point of the season and their first point away from home since January 2003.

The first half, by the standards of Shire v Albion Rovers matches, was electrifying, with goals raining in from all angles. But neither team could maintain that sort of effort or marksmanship and the second half subsided into dour defending and some desperate clearances. Ross Donaldson, who also lives locally, produced one of his better games but was booked 'for unsporting behaviour' (i.e. he kicked his marker up in the air) and banned for the next match.

The home fans found a draw against the Shire hard to take and finally turned their wrath on their own players.

'If that's the best you can gi' us, youse can go fuck your-selves,' cried one.

'Thank fuck it's the Scotland game next week and we can have a Saturday off,' cried another, with slightly more subtlety.

The international was against Norway at Hampden and Shaggy, being the only Norwegian playing football in

Scotland, was suddenly in demand. He was interviewed on radio at Firs Park training in the week before the game – an interview that went swimmingly until Chris Miller sneaked up and pulled his shorts down. The midfielder also delivered some outspoken comments about the standard of training at the Shire compared to the Third Division in Norway at which listener Dennis Newall blew his top.

Shaggy, bravely, went along to Hampden in Norway colours, and even more bravely sat in the midst of the Tartan Army on the terraces. He even got up and cheered when Norway scored. 'Well, for half a second, then I quickly sat down again. I'm not that crazy.'

Training nights at Firs Park were an education in themselves. The manager would invariably have to deal with a string of disaffected players, usually led by The Cat, who had been left out for the last three games and was totally pissed off. Dennis explained as patiently as possible that The Cat was a valued member of the squad, that it was a sixteen-man game these days and that if he took the trouble to work on his shite kicking he might improve his chances.

Training consisted of one-lap sprints at three-quarter pace round the perimeter and some heading practice. The keepers would be away in a world of their own, supplying crosses to each other. The walking wounded would be doing press-ups on the benches in the changing room urged on by David Jenkins in best army PTI mode: 'Get your arse down lower,' he'd tell Ross Donaldson.

Jimmy Wilson revealed he had a tractor mower on loan, much to the delight of Daft Dougie. His days of toil with the lawn mower were over. Jimmy couldn't get Dougie off the tractor. Even in the rain.

Back in his office, Dennis Newall offered me a list of league managers who were going to get the sack. He was so full of ambition, but in a nice way. The manager of Linlithgow Rose had been spouting off about how he should get a senior job. Dennis was scornful. His position was getting more secure by the match, but he was still a hard man to satisfy.

Montrose, one of the teams hard on the heels of Gretna and Peterhead, had arrived at Firs Park expecting to win. But the Shire got stuck into them from the start. Joe Robertson's goal was deserved but, despite Newall's half-time warnings about the dangers of losing concentration, they lost their momentum a bit and Montrose came back into it. The home defending became more and more desperate and with seven minutes left and the Shire within touching distance of their first three points of the season, Montrose won a free-kick twenty yards out and their winger scored.

Dennis's inquest at the end was completely drowned out by the celebrations from next door. Montrose had got out of jail. A defeat against the Shire was an awful thing to contemplate, but it was a sign of the Shire's heightened expectations that a 1-1 draw was now seen in as bad a light as their more usual defeat. 'See defending like that,' said Newall. 'You see some of that shite we have to put up with? It's enough to drive a man to drink.' I headed off to the pub in total agreement.

THE LOST WEEKEND

'To travel hopefully is a better thing than to arrive', wrote Robert Louis Stevenson. The Edinburgh-born bard was probably a supporter of Hearts or Hibernian, but he could well have had East Stirlingshire away fixtures in mind.

We would always set off in a mood of expectation, for sportsmen of every description are optimists by definition and the Shire players and management are no exception. Once Mr Bryan and his bus pulled up outside Firs Park and we had loaded on board the various kit bags, spare footballs, training cones and Dennis's magnetic tactics' board, someone would put on a video, or we'd listen dreamily to Radio One.

There would be the laddish piss-taking and leery boasting about the previous evening's activities, characteristic of every football team in transit together. Some even slept. The management team would discuss the day's game-plan and Alex Forsyth, in splendid isolation in the tour guide's seat, would read the *Daily Mail* aloud to himself. Les Thomson would catch up on his chief executive's business which involved, in the main, the opening of large bills from Scottish Water or Scottish Power, and I would take in the scenery.

But, an hour out from the opposition's stadium, no matter whose, the mood would change dramatically. Invariably, if I glanced behind at that moment, every player would be gazing out of the window in rapt introspection, seeing nothing but thinking a lot. And, of course, a lot of the time it would have been far better had we never arrived.

By the time of the first of the two trips to Gretna, in October, I had begun to wonder what a winning football coach looked and sounded like. I longed for the hearty ring of young men's laughter (the justification for any sport), the sight of Dennis Newall and Greig Denham with their arms around each other, and the merry crack of Tennents ring-pull cans. True, we had managed that mind-boggling draw at Albion Rovers, a result that earned the first Littlewoods bonus and ended a run of eleven successive defeats, but that hardly counted. It wasn't even a proper away trip.

Les Thomson had a firmly defined ordinance on what constituted a journey worthy of employing Mr Bryan at £1,000 a go. Peterhead and Elgin up in the far north-east qualified, as did Gretna on the English border and Montrose, up in the wilds of Angus. Queen's Park, who play at Glasgow's Hampden Park, home of the national team, just crept in by Les's mileage calculations. But for every other away fixture, the players travelled independently in their own cars, often shared.

At many games, the first sight of their team-mates since the Thursday training was when they arrived at the away ground. It seemed hardly the best way to engender team spirit, the often artificially created sense of pulling together on which every successful team thrives. There would be late cry-offs, too, usually for midweek or evening fixtures and, on the memorably awful trip to Gretna on 16 October, we even missed picking up one player altogether.

Sod's Law is the inevitability that fate will occasionally throw dollops of perversity at humankind: you will always cut yourself shaving if you are late for an important appointment; the place you are looking for will always be on the page fold of the *A to Z*, the adverts will always be on when you change TV channels, the Guinness will always run out just when you get to the bar. And, if you allow two hours and fifteen minutes for a journey of two hours and fifteen minutes, and it is raining heavily to boot, there are going to be hold-ups. Shire's Law, we should call it.

I had a feeling it wasn't going to be our day halfway down the M74 when someone consulted the team sheet and realised we were a player short. A swift head-count revealed that the Shire squad, already ravaged by the suspension of Ross Donaldson (for being shown too many yellow cards, although some said he had done a Beckham and booked himself out of the Gretna trip deliberately) and injury, was indeed another man down.

'No panic,' said Les Thomson. We were due to pick up a trialist on the way. No one knew what he looked like, but that wouldn't be a problem because the driver would recognise the club tracksuit. Unfortunately, A. Trialist hadn't been issued with his uniform and we drove straight past him. Someone later recalled seeing a sodden figure waiting by the roadside. He may still be there for all I know.

Just outside Bothwell, the Scottish Executive warning signs flashed up our worst fears: a huge tailback of traffic gridlocked in the Lanarkshire countryside. The choice was a long wait in the hope that the logjam would eventually clear, or the scenic route through the Clyde Valley. Having travelled half a mile in forty minutes, Mr Bryan and Les Thomson put Plan B into action and we turned off at Abington to head down The Road of a Thousand Garden Centres.

Half the tourists in the western world – eager to take in the delights of the Lanarkshire orchards, the hunting lodge of Chatelherault and the David Livingstone Centre at Blantyre – had had precisely the same idea. Our progress became first stately, and then slowed to a crawl. The occasional farm tractor and milk wagon did not help. Les Thomson turned ashen-faced with anxiety. Even Alex Forsyth put down his *Daily Mail* as he began to absorb the implications of our non-arrival and the prospect of the game being postponed. Dennis Newall, for his part, took it all in his stride: 'If the game is called off,' he reasoned, looking back on two draws in succession, 'I could be in line for Manager of the Month.'

I thought of the swingeing fine, the severe embarrassment of a no-show, but Les consoled: 'The Scottish Football League can't fine us if we have set off,' he said. By now I was beginning to get the picture. Someone, I think it was Stuart Cosgrove, had once told me that if there was a god of creation then there must be a separate god for Scottish football clubs. 'How else could they survive?' he had asked. If he was right, the Shire must have done something to upset that god. Their ill fortune was almost mythical.

Thomson couldn't get a signal on his mobile to inform his Gretna counterpart that we were delayed and, with cruel irony, the Radio One DJ chose the moment to play *Is This the Way to Amarillo?* On the outskirts of Gretna there was a further delay when a white Rolls Royce, bearing a canoodling couple and a sign that read 'Just Married', pulled out in front of us. The driver, oblivious to the red faces and effing and blinding behind, proceeded down the road in the direction of the Old Blacksmith's Shop Inc. at around ten miles an hour. We arrived at Raydale Park, to derisive hoots from the gathered Gretna fans, twenty minutes before the kick-off.

Dennis now had a problem. His pre-match routine, home and away, seldom varied: arrival ninety minutes before a three o'clock kick-off, first pep-talk in the dressing room with the players still in their suits, cigar outside while they changed, then individual talks with individual players while they warmed up. Finally winding up, at around seven minutes to three, with his familiar incitements to 'be men', 'that lot next door are all shite' and, more and more frequently as the season wore on, 'alleviate the pain'.

Plainly, all this was not possible at Gretna. He wouldn't even have time for a smoke and his routine was thrown out still further by the appearance of the referee in the away dressing room. He had put the kick-off back for fifteen minutes, but then complicated matters more by informing the management and players that the Shire were to line up before the start and brandish an individual red card in the air, this being part of the SFL's recently launched campaign against the country's football bigots. 'Red Card against Racism', they had called it.

So, instead of a team talk, the baffled Shire players had to be told what the red cards were all about, why they had been issued with them and where, and when to raise them in the air. But Newall was left with just enough time to say: 'Gretna will be pissed off with all the waiting around. Really pissed off. We could catch them cold. Literally'.

And so it proved. After six minutes the full-back David Harvey crossed from the right and striker Derek Ure pounced, amid a deathly silence, to put the Shire ahead. This was not in the script.

After that, the game became like a visit to the dentist – you just prayed for it all to be over. Like the M74, it was one-way traffic. Gretna equalised in the twenty-eighth minute when a short free-kick was pushed into the path of full-back Mark Birch, who smashed a low twenty-five-yard shot into the bottom corner. Gretna went in front just two minutes later when they broke from a Shire corner, and Ryan Baldacchino, a noisome little winger with a collection of multi-coloured boots and a step-over like Manchester United's Christian Ronaldo, clipped a cross to the far post for Bryan Gilfillan to thump in a header from close range. Gretna's moving statue, a monolithic centre-forward called Kenny Deuchar – the scourge of Third Division defences – grabbed the first of a hat-trick, to make it 3-1 in the thirty-ninth minute when Gilfillan chipped into the box and he headed in.

It was turning into an awful afternoon for Greig Denham, the only Shire player to match Deuchar in height, and the obvious man to mark him. With Gretna now nicely warmed up, it was 4-1 just two minutes later when Deuchar, again, climbed high above Denham to head a Baldacchino cross in off the underside of the bar. With the Shire defence by then looking like accommodating traffic cops, David Bingham played in Gavin Skelton to drill the fifth home nine minutes into the second half.

The torment went on. Bingham cleverly flicked on a Birch cross and Deuchar had his hat-trick. His replacement, Brian Wake, then appeared and we could all guess what was coming. Sure enough, the substitute made it 7-1 with eight minutes to go after Ross Gilpin had spilled another shot. Baldacchino, with footwork slick as Fred Astaire's, finished things off with the eighth. A nine-goal thriller, as Des Lynam would say.

More goals, in fact, than Shire fans. Just eight, including Ure's mother and younger brother, had made the trip from Falkirk. They were reinforced by a dozen English fans from Wigan who had, weirdly, adopted the Shire as their 'other' team. The Falkirk contingent was further depleted just after half-time when two of them were ejected from the home end by a battalion of no-nonsense stewards. The genteel burghers of Gretna, apparently, had been upset by an outbreak of *lingua franca* from the visiting fans when the fourth goal went in.

Back in the away dressing room the recriminations began. Gilpin was an obvious target but could really be blamed for only one goal, when he allowed a speculative shot to slip through his fingers. The defence bore the brunt of the manager's assault and we all waited in trepidation as Newall berated Nos. 2, 3 and 4.

Greig Denham had played at No. 5 and Deuchar had had a field day. Dennis Newall had known Greig for eleven years, since the latter was seventeen and 'the hardest wee bastard I have ever come across'. Dennis waded straight in.

'Greig, were you dreaming out there?'

'What the fuck do you mean?'

'Their centre-forward. He's a bag of shite. I could run faster than him and I'm fifty-one years old. I could run backwards faster than him. What's more, I wouldn't have given him the space you gave him.'

'Well, maybe you should have fucking played then.'

The manager, scarlet with anger and frustration, moved on. The midfield had been absent without leave; Grant Findlay, the teenage striker, had fallen over his own feet when clear on goal; Ure had taken his goal well but had failed to close down the Gretna defenders. 'You all think you've arrived,' he told them. 'You want the Ferrari before you've got the licence. I tell you something, if you can't find some fucking pride and start to play like men, I'll get some in who can.' I was never sure, to be honest, where those 'some' might come from. But I kept quiet.

In the players' lounge, later, Deuchar had a firm grip of the match ball. It was his to keep. His habit of scoring hat-tricks – six in the season to equal an ancient record held by Jimmy Greaves – must have made another sizeable hole in Brooks Mileson's budget.

We arrived home to a deserted Firs Park at ten o'clock that night. Saturday was dead, although for one man the night was still young. Mr Bryan had hardly pulled on the hand brake when Alex Forsyth was on his feet, down the steps and off at a run in the direction of the retail park.

'He's off line-dancing,' explained his son-in-law proudly. 'It's great, isn't it? Seventy-five and just look at him. He's at it every Saturday night and every Monday night.'

'But what about the Monday board meetings?'

'He asked for them to be switched to Tuesdays.' Someone told me later that 'he likes partners about six feet tall so he can stick his nose in their tits.'

Despite my scepticism, as he had promised in the wake of the Gretna massacre, Dennis Newall immediately began to look for fresh blood. The January transfer window was two months away and it appeared likely that the only incomers he would find would come from the junior ranks, or no-hope trialists. Even Patrick from County Clare could be in with a shout.

But he surprised us all. A week after Gretna, via their insider trader at Firs Park, Gordon Parks, the *Daily Record* announced: 'SHIRE WANT GAZZA!' This certainly was big news. Just when we thought that the famous former England footballer had hit rock bottom, he was apparently prepared to sink even lower.

At first I put this down to fanciful reporting, in newspaper terms what is known as a 'flier', whereby a sports editor without a worthwhile story to put on the next day's back page will simply ask a reporter to make something up. Such stories invariably contain a kernel of truth. A reporter may, during a conversation with, let's say, Graeme Souness, come up with something along the lines of: 'That Ronaldhino, some player, eh Graeme?'

'Oh, yes, the best in the world I would say.'

'Betcha'd like him at St James Park?'

'Of course. Any club would want a player like that. But let's get real. He has a three-year contract at Barcelona and we haven't got that sort of money. Now, do you want the team for Saturday?'

Next day, the world, and no doubt a somewhat nonplussed Graeme Souness, would wake to a back page headline that read: 'Magpies go for Ronaldhino!' The little matter of the player's contract and the several million pounds that Newcastle didn't have would not, it goes without saying, merit a mention.

But I knew Parks had the ear of Newall, and vice versa. It was Parks who had persuaded his fellow Weegie, Joe Robertson, to sign for the Shire when he could plainly have got a better job elsewhere. And Newall did appear to be serious.

Gazza's last club, Boston United, he reasoned, was not too far removed in the way of facilities, playing strength and performance to the Shire. And it was believed that Gascoigne – who had recently followed the precedent of the Artist Formerly Known as Prince and changed his name to G8 – may also have had some mates left in the west of Scotland from his time at Rangers. He might welcome the chance to catch up with them, said the manager.

But his unshakeable conviction that G8 could decide to end his career at Firs Park was based on what he saw as one piece of inescapable logic: 'He's done dafter things in his life.' I thought back on G8's life and career – the alcoholism, the depression, the reported domestic violence, even the multiple failed football comebacks with minor teams. Then I thought of the Shire. 'Dennis, I don't think so,' I said, as kindly as possible. But in many ways Gascoigne and the

Shire were a match made in heaven; both dogged by bad luck, self-destruction and surviving on past history.

Since leaving Rangers in 1998 after three seasons in Glasgow, G8's career had subsided rapidly. He went to Middlesbrough, where former England team-mate Bryan Robson gave him a free transfer, and in the summer of 2000 his old boss from his Ibrox days, Walter Smith, signed him for Everton. Perhaps wisely, Smith ensured that the one-year contract Gascoigne signed contained a slew of clauses aimed at protecting the club from embarrassment should Gazza get up to his old tricks again.

Sure enough, an alcoholic binge at the tail end of the 2000/1 season prompted a spell in an Arizona cold turkey clinic and a persistent thigh injury ended his season. When Smith was fired at the end of the next season, Gazza's Goodison days were numbered and it was all downhill from there.

He joined Burnley for the rest of the season, before heading for China. Like the Shire, when fate sensed that a man was down, it began to put the boot in. The SARS virus scare, which crippled the Chinese football calendar, left him high and dry again and in July 2004 he joined Boston in a player–coach role. After just three months and four league appearances in South Lincolnshire, Gazza had had enough.

Now, like so many fallen footballers with famous names, he was in demand less for his fading playing ability and more for the marketing possibilities his name afforded him. As Brazil's World Cup-winning captain Socrates found at Garforth Town in England's Northern Counties East League, and George Best discovered at Bournemouth, there is a booming market for football has-beens. Someone, some-where, will always be willing to pay you just for turning up. It's called putting bums on seats.

In the case of G8, there was one obvious stumbling block: how would a man who in his prime earned £25,000 a week react when Chairman Mackin told him: 'Well, son, we pay a tenner a week here. I like you, but I am not going to break that rule for anyone'? Newall, however, with his marketing and sales background, had worked that one out, too. 'We're sponsored by Littlewoods, aren't we? They could find two grand a week for a couple of months. Think of the publicity they would get. The club would benefit from the massive gates. Think of all the media attention. Think of the shirt sales.' I was – even if every Shire fan bought one that would add up to, well, 250 shirts.

The G8 deal certainly made it big in the Scottish newspapers, although only one, the story's originators, appeared to give it any sort of credence. The others tried to knock it down, as rivals do. Gascoigne, the *Daily Record* revealed, would be at Firs Park for the Peterhead match, weigh things up, and then come to a decision. In the end, he never showed, although a helicopter buzzing overhead at around 2.45 p.m. sparked a flutter of optimism in the home support. The chopper, however, continued in the general direction of Grangemouth, hotly pursued by a large pink pig, and it was back to sober reality.

The news of G8's imminent arrival, oddly, had had little positive effect on the home gate. Most of the Scottish newspapers had given up on the idea and the press box was empty apart from Tad (for the *Falkirk Herald*) and a writer from the *Press and Journal*, Peterhead's local paper. And it wasn't just the reporters who were missing. The Blue Toon were riding high in Division Three; they were on a roll. Promotion was beckoning. The absence of travelling fans was puzzling.

All was revealed by Les Thomson, whose single phone line

had turned hot an hour or so before the match with calls from desperate visiting fans all asking the same question: 'Where the fuck is Firs Park?' Most of them were in Stirling, having assumed that a club called East Stirlingshire would be based there.

This, apparently, was a common occurrence. Thomson could justifiably have invested in an answerphone with a recorded message saying: 'This is Firs Park, the home of East Stirlingshire FC. If you are currently in Stirling, take the M9 south and etc., etc. . . .' Most of the Peterhead fans, thankfully for them, arrived in time to see their team win 2-1 and maintain their 100 per cent success rate against the Shire.

The Shire managed a sterling defensive performance for the first forty-five minutes before the familiar failings re-surfaced. The Cat, back in favour after the Gretna debacle, unwisely left his line to cut out a cross from the Peterhead full-back, but failed to go far enough and Martin Bavidge nodded the ball over the keeper's flailing arms and towards the empty goal. Fellow striker Scott Michie arrived before any Shire defenders to tap the ball over the line.

Steven Oates then gave away a penalty which not even Dennis Newall could argue about and Michie easily beat The Cat from the spot. 'Oatesy, you are fucking killing us,' bawled Newall. Oates, who was only twenty, was a physically gifted defender but raw as mustard seed. Newall and Denham spent too much time on the sidelines trying to drum in the basics. 'Oatesy, stay goalside of your man, for fuck's sake.' 'Oatesy, stay tight on him.' In one game Denham even had to show him how to steal a few yards at a throw-in, an instinct I had always believed that footballers inherited at birth.

But Oatesy wasn't the only one struggling. Denham had made another comeback, but again ran out of puff and had to be substituted at half-time. The manager, to Greig's unconcealed delight, was then banished to the stand by a referee wearied by the constant criticism from the home dugout and, ironically, the Shire suddenly began to play. Ross Donaldson did a stately topple in the box and Joe Robertson stroked in the penalty to set up an exciting, but fruitless, finish.

The schism between the manager and his assistant appeared to have widened after Greig's bollocking at Gretna. On the way back up the M74 Denham had refused to speak to his friend and had arrived for the Peterhead match in his own car, instead of Dennis's BMW. He was responsible for the first Peterhead goal and when he was pulled off at half-time, he came back to the dugout close to tears. 'I'm getting far too old for this,' choked the twenty-eight year old.

The hypothetical question that plagued me, still does, was this: would Gazza have dragged the Shire youngsters up towards his level, or would he have sunk to theirs? And if he did, would Dennis have called him a fucking c**t to his face? We were never to know. An hour or so after the Peterhead defeat the manager received a text from one of the Littlewoods representatives: 'Gazza,' it read, 'is not interested.'

The arguments about whether G8 had seriously considered a whole new chapter of his career at Firs Park, or whether it was simply a clever publicity stunt, have never been resolved. All I can say is that driving back from Falkirk to Edinburgh that same night I was overtaken by a black Series 7 BMW close to the M8/M9 interchange. The driver was doing close to 100 m.p.h. and the passenger was leaning over the backseat shouting into his ear. I couldn't see their faces, but could hardly miss the personalised number plate. G8. Maybe I was seeing things for, as most Scottish football writers will tell you, a working Saturday can be a sore trial at times.

Fridays in the two major publishing centres of Glasgow and Edinburgh are traditionally Nights of the Big Swally. Thirsty hacks gather in the Jinglin' Geordie, the Press Bar or The Bon Accord and get stuck in big-time. Saturday mornings are invariably given over to desperate recovery, with all the problems that can bring. 'Delirium tremens: a severe psychotic condition common to heavy drinkers and one that often causes vivid hallucinations'.

In Ray Milland's case it was the bat making a meal of the mouse in the ceiling of that New York drunk tank; in my case it was the sight of Bob the Builder, a pith-helmeted Lt Harry Faversham, a Keystone Cop, three Mexican bandits carrying blow-up sex dolls and a six-foot-high yellow banana staggering out of the Gordon Arms at around ten to three on the Saturday afternoon after my G8 sighting. All were heading in the direction of Firs Park, Falkirk.

A large proportion of the staff of lads' mag *Loaded* had been flown up from London for a day at the expense of Littlewoods, who share the same PR company. They had decided to make a day of it. This was their first sight of the Shire and the majority were Arsenal supporters, so it could be said they were slumming it to an extent, but since they had spent most of the morning in the pub, by three o'clock they were immune to the culture shock. All, in fact, were in good mood and voice, although initially unsure which team they should be shouting for.

Littlewoods had opened the Firs Park gates for free, so there was a healthy attendance of around 600. Everyone seemed happy about this, except the overworked Firs Park stewards who hadn't had to deal with multitudes like this before. There was talk about 'segregating the punters' with duct tape, or even calling in police reinforcements. In fact all the punters, whether from Cowdenbeath, Falkirk or Darn

Sarth mingled happily. And, despite their geographical demarcations and varied accents, they did have one thing in common: they were all pissed.

True, there was some of the banter associated with rival supporters, particularly those from Scotland and those who followed the 'Auld Enemy'. The Cowdenbeath fans chanted 'Cockney gits', 'Leave it aht' or 'Strike a light, guv' at regular intervals and the visitors responded in kind with: 'Up yer kilt, you Jock bastards' or 'Go and shag a sheep'.

In the home dressing room, another hallucination: the chairman was making a rare appearance. He dug me in the ribs, whacked me across the shoulders and warned me, not for the first time: 'Now, don't be giving me pelters in that book of yours, Jeff. I like you, by the way.' Then, after Dennis Newall had, once again, introduced him to the players and delivered his tactical master plan about the importance of playing down the channels and keeping a shape, Mackin did his Henry V: 'Let's leave some of those Cowdenbeath bastards in cement,' he crooned.

They did their best, but Cowdenbeath were not in the mood to be consigned to a pillar on an M9 flyover. Greig Denham, plainly struggling, had to be subbed at half-time for the second week in succession and The Cat, granted another life, had another of his mixed days in goal. He saved a couple of early Cowdenbeath efforts, but was off his line and stranded when a header looped over him for their opening goal. A header from the now work-permitted Shaggy went narrowly wide of the upright before a sweeping three-man move tore the home defence to shreds for the opening goal.

After that the Shire seemed to surrender the midfield. The second goal came after fifty-five minutes and for the first time I noticed a curious phenomenon common to many

Shire fans: while most supporters leave five minutes before the final whistle when their team are losing, the Shire's head for the Firs Park exits at around the hour mark. Perhaps they should get in for half-price.

The lads and lasses from *Loaded*, too, with the effects of their earlier carousing slowly wearing off, disappeared long before the end, leaving a large empty banana skin flapping symbolically in the breeze on the turnstile end corner flag.

As I drove past the Gordon Lounge on the way back to Edinburgh, the Keystone Cop, armed with what looked like a giant black dildo, was chasing Bob the Builder around the car park watched by the man in the pith helmet and two of the Mexicans. Maybe it was time to stop drinking.

6 DAY OF THE DOUGHNUTS

Mackin was back in Scotland a week later, this time to face the music at the club AGM. Or, as the minutes had it: to present his annual report at the East Stirlingshire Football and Athletic Club shareholders' meeting.

I found the venue, the three-star Park Lodge, on Camelon Road, overlooking one of Falkirk's few green bits, Dollar Park. The chairman, with his assembled board, met me close by reception. Alex Forsyth, accompanied by his son-in-law, was in best truculent troll mode and across the other side of the lobby a group of Shire supporters, Ian Ramsay among them, muttered among themselves in a tight, conspiratorial group. The two factions eyeballed each other with open hostility. The mood was similar to that before a prize fight.

'You'll have a laugh tonight,' Mackin told me. 'Did I tell you I like you, Jeff?' I had actually begun to quite like him, too. He was big, he blustered, and he was quite scary. But he was open, almost artless – albeit in the confrontational way of many Glaswegians. Friends for life, enemies for a whole lot longer.

The club had splashed out for one of the conference suites, and the hotel staff had arranged around 100 seats in the body of the hall facing an elevated stage on which stood a table and six more chairs. It looked like a school assembly. Or a scene from *Judgement at Nuremberg*.

Most football club AGMs are defined, like everything else in sports reportage, by cliché. If games have two halves, managers insist, at the end of the day, that the season has a long way to go, and playmakers spread the ball about, then AGMs are always, always, stormy affairs. Given the background of conflict and enmity between the chairman and the groundswell support of the Shire, it goes without saying that theirs were stormier than most. Dissent and controversy were written into the history of Shire annual general meetings. The 2004 version had a lot to live up to.

Four years earlier, the then vice-chairman, a Falkirk businessman called Lex Miller, had announced that his re-election had been blocked by Mackin. Later, Miller was to claim that he had been ousted because: 'I was bringing money into the club, something the chairman didn't want to do.' As he went on to turn Sauchie Juniors into one of Scotland's best non-league sides before joining the board of Falkirk, it could be said that he had the last laugh.

In 2001, it had been Alex Forsyth's turn to throw a wobbly over the appointment of Douglas Morrison on to the board and, although the 2003 AGM had passed in relative calm and order, it did begin in high farce. The assembled shareholders had scarcely settled in their seats before Tad Kopszywa demanded that the proceedings should be declared unconstitutional as he had not received his notice calling the meeting.

Tad, who does own shares and was also there to report on the meeting for the *Falkirk Herald*, had wanted it stopped before it began. Perhaps he fancied a night off. In the end he withdrew his objection. The traditional vote on whether the press should be allowed to be present for the duration of the meeting followed. Tad, the only reporter present, voted for himself to remain.

A year on, the Shire had made little progress in any direction. They were still waiting for a first win, the largesse of Littlewoods had made minimal difference, Gazza had declined to come on board and the ground had been sold against the wishes of the majority of the fans. Now those fans, righteous indignation written all over their faces even before the meeting was called to order, were going to have their say. At seven o'clock precisely, and with much smacking of lips, we filed into a room in which the atmosphere was charged with anticipation.

Looking at the list of shareholders provided by Companies House, it was at once clear that whatever was said, or proposed, from the floor of the meeting would make little difference to Mackin and his board.

In December 2003, the nominal value of each share was twenty-five pence and some 8,000 had been issued at a total value of £2,000. The 8,000 were spread through an eclectic bunch of people, ranging from Labour MSP Dennis Canavan, who had fifteen at the time, to Mr Willie Watson of Wellington, on the North Island of New Zealand, who held four. In all, there were around 350 shareholders listed, twenty-four of whom had made it to the 2004 AGM.

Fortunately, apologies were received from only three, one being Canavan, the MP for Falkirk West, who had more pressing matters to attend to. There was a brief hiatus when the vote was taken on whether Mr Tadek Kopszywa be allowed to remain and report on proceedings. Not surprisingly, Tad, twirling like a dervish in his excitement, once again duly voted in favour. Then, to the symbolic sound of the bell at hotel reception ringing in the distance, they waded in.

Les Mitchell, the Firs Park DJ and announcer and, like his father before him, a lifelong Shire fan and shareholder, kicked off with a sneaky question directed at the chairman. Exactly how many matches had he attended that season? This was a bit of a blow below the belt as Mitchell made a point of conducting a public head count on the number of directors present at home matches, and plainly knew the answer.

Mackin got to his feet, chewed his fingernail, thought for a time, then replied: 'Are you asking me?'

'Yes, Mr Chairman, I am asking you.' 'Aye, well, most of the work I do for the Shire is during the week. You don't see the half of what I do. Because I'm no' at matches doesn't mean I'm no' pulling my weight.'

'And what do you do during the week, Mr Chairman?'

'Well, er, I run the club.' Alex Forsyth, seated alongside John Morton at the opposite end of the table, snorted derisively. Morton shook his head.

There were questions on the appointment of Dennis Newall as head coach. Davie Sneddon, the veteran former Kilmarnock manager, had been the other contender on the shortlist of two and was probably better qualified. But he had virtually disqualified himself by asking for £70 a week, wages or expenses. Newall had asked for nothing. That, said Mackin, made commercial sense. 'Aye, but I didnae vote for him,' shouted Alex Forsyth. Alec McCabe outlined the details of the sale of Firs Park and confirmed that it had gone for £1.3m. 'I didnae vote for that, either,' shouted Forsyth.

Suddenly, just to my left, a large bespectacled man with a round, red face rose to his feet and addressed the assembled board. 'Doughnuts, you are doughnuts,' he shouted. The room went silent. Morton and Forsyth nodded their approval. Mackin looked remarkably sanguine, almost as if he had been expecting this.

'You,' went on the interloper, turning towards Douglas

Morrison. 'When are you going to say something? What exactly are you doing here? Have you no tongue in your head. Let's hear you say something.' Morrison blinked, smiled his secretive smile, and said nothing. 'I'm going to your school in Greenock to tell them what sort of a man you are.'

'And you,' this time to McCabe. 'You got me bankrupted, Alec McCabe. I saw your name on the letters. You are all going to sell this club down the pan. I know for a fact you've already sold the grandstand to Falkirk rugby club.'

The meeting had now disintegrated into total disorder. There were shouts of support for the interloper from the floor and more shouts of 'I didnae vote for that' from Forsyth. McCabe shook his head and tut-tutted; Mackin smiled broadly. It was the smile of a man who knew the day was won; he was on familiar territory now.

'Ross, you are now on a yellow card,' he told his assailant, whose face was now purple with rage.

'No, I'm not. I am giving myself a red card.'

With that he marched towards the door, pausing only to deliver his punchline: 'You are all a bunch of doughnuts! Good night, doughnuts!'

After that, there wasn't a lot left to say. There was enough time for Forsyth and Morton to be re-elected to the board unopposed before, with a fan midway through a speech about how much the Shire meant to him, Mackin called the meeting to a close. The whole affair had lasted one hour and fifteen minutes and for sheer entertainment value had surpassed any football match.

But I couldn't help recall the film *Cool Hand Luke* and the words of the prison boss after his guards had beaten up Paul Newman for the twelfth time: 'What we've got here is a failure to communicate.'

The rabble-rouser was a former vice-chairman (Shire vice-chairs seem to have a chaotic history) called Ross Strang. Strang, along with the then chairman George Ronald, had been a casualty of Mackin's messy takeover five years previously. They had attempted to keep out the Mackin cabal, the case had gone to court and they lost. They had also been ordered to pay costs, had been unable or unwilling to do so, and had been declared bankrupt. Strang lost his Falkirk newsagent's business. It would be true to say there was bad blood there.

But Strang still had at least two allies on the Shire board. Four days after the Day of the Doughnuts we climbed on the bus bound for the long trip to Elgin to find the former vice-chairman already on board. He was seated just behind Alex Forsyth, smiling broadly, and in friendly conversation with John Morton. I got the picture: powerless to outvote Mackin, they had decided simply to thumb their noses at him.

The chairman, of course, wasn't travelling, but we still had to pick up his earthbound representative, Les Thomson, at his home in Larbert. The chief executive climbed on all cheery bonhomie; Strang hid his face in the *Guardian*. When Thomson did finally turn round half an hour into the journey, to find the florid face of Strang staring back at him, you could say it made the day for both of them.

It had been a bad morning for Thomson. The *Daily Record* had carried a story, byline Gordon Parks, about the Firs Park floodlights failing at Thursday's training. The players, so Parks alleged – and he should know as he was there with them – had been forced to play a practice game in a Falkirk municipal park ... with car headlights trained on them. The players on the bus, most of them avid *Record* or *Sun* readers, had a good chortle at this.

Confronted by the *agent provocateur* on the bus, Les kept his mouth shut, but was plainly thinking plenty. At the midjourney break, he pointedly refused to sit on the same table as Strang and, instead, ushered me into the empty seat alongside the AGM wrecker while he sat with the players. The Shire's former vice-chairman immediately slipped me a piece of paper with his home phone number on it and offered to 'spill the beans'.

We had called at Aviemore, to find that football had taken over *The Chalet Café*, much to the disgust of its wait-ress – the stroppy sort endemic in the Blackpool of the Highlands. A band of cheerful fans from Bo'ness, on the way up to Lossiemouth for their OVD Junior Cup second-round tie, were on the next table and there was much mutual well-wishing. They served also as a sobering reminder that at every level of Scottish football, the Shire are the have-nots.

The Bo'ness players had stayed overnight at a hotel in Grantown-on-Spey. This, said one of their followers, a middle-aged woman with two children, was the reason for the club's fine team spirit. On match days, she continued, the team assembled at their home ground – Newtown Park – and trav-elled together on a team bus, even for fixtures only two or three miles away. 'There's nae cliques at our club,' she pointed out proudly. 'They're all in it together. Everyone pulls for everyone else.'

The Shire could never be accused of that. At Elgin's Borough Briggs ground, as the players made the ritual pre-match examination of the playing surface, the factions were obvious. The Glasgow wide boys (Gordon Parks, Johnny Walker and Joe Robertson) grouped in their own wisecracking, irreverent huddle; the goalkeepers hung together, lost in thought, wondering which of them would spend the after-noon under siege; and there were separate little gatherings for the club's old hands who had survived the new man-ager's purge, and for the nervous young reserves. The two college boys, Shaggy and Scott Livingstone, had their own, small, cerebral confab.

But, as the season had progressed, I had learned to recognise positive vibes. The atmosphere in the away dressing room at Borough Briggs that day was just right; not too quiet, not too loud. And, after all, weren't these our fall guys? The fall guys were comparative newcomers to Scottish senior football, although Elgin's Highland League credentials were unimpeachable.

Like Berwick, much of their mystique in the eyes of their fans was built on gallant underdogs' performances in the Scottish Cup. In 1960, they were narrowly beaten at home by a Celtic side approaching their European Cup-winning pomp, and in 1968 they had reached the quarter-finals. In 1977, much of the north-east of Scotland travelled to Elgin to see them beaten 3–0 by Rangers after another rewarding Cup run. They had joined the league in 2000/1, but had never gained higher than sixth place.

Their playing fortunes were in the hands of one of the most iconic of Scottish players, Davie Robertson, who had arrived in March 2003. Robertson had started an illustrious career as a youngster with Aberdeen alongside Alex McLeish, Willie Miller and Stewart McKimmie, and under the management of Alex Ferguson before Glasgow Rangers signed him in 1991 for £900,000.

Leeds United paid over £1m for Robertson before, like Greig Denham's, his career was ended by cruciate ligament damage. The two of them could compare medical notes and commiserate about the vagaries of fate that had taken Denham to the Shire and Robertson to Borough Briggs, a ground that had been opened in 1921 and hadn't changed much since.

Elgin, being in the north-east of Scotland, offered another opportunity for Dennis Newall to prime his troops with the sheep shaggers' speech, but this venue was subtly different from Peterhead. The fans, many of whom arrived in Barbours and flat caps, turned out to be unnaturally civilised. Lacking the one-eyed insularity that distinguishes most football support, they seemed fair and, occasionally, even appreciative of the opposition, and the referee.

'Finlay, didn't you think that East Stirlingshire player was just a tad offside?' one demanded of his companion in the seats behind me.

'To be fair to the match official, Hamish,' replied his friend. 'I think the referee may be experiencing difficulty in picking up signals from his linesman due to the fact that some of the match stewards in the stand on that side of the pitch are wearing similar fluorescent yellow tops.'

The home support had little to shout about anyway, as the Shire outplayed Elgin totally. I'll repeat that because I love the sound of it. The Shire outplayed Elgin totally. The outcome never seemed in doubt, even after the Shire went a goal behind.

Ross Donaldson enjoyed one of his better days and even Dennis Newall never mentioned his alleged squatter's rights at Burger King during the half-time interval. The striker had a header cleared off the line and he twice went close to scoring. The most notable effort came when he found space and shot just narrowly over from twenty yards. But the opening goal just would not come and, typically of the Shire, shoddy defending allowed Elgin to go ahead. This time, however, the Shire's heads did not go down.

The college boys' clique – Livingstone's cross, Shaggy's header – combined for the equaliser. Shaggy scored a second and a fantastic strike by man of the match Joe Robertson settled it. At the final whistle, the small band of travelling fans hesitated a split second before cavorting across the terraces in celebration. They could hardly believe their eyes.

It had been a horribly disjointed match, with over thirty fouls, but nobody cared. For the first time in living memory the journey home was on a happy Bryan's bus. We stopped at the supermarket just round the corner from the ground for a carry-out funded by the pools company. Cans of beer fizzed behind us, Dennis Newall and Greig Denham exchanged high fives, John Morton chortled, Alex Forsyth smiled into his *Daily Mail*. Ross Strang grinned at Les, Les grinned right back. At last, we were one big happy, winning clique.

November, the month when club secretaries traditionally start to hark unto Heather the Weather on BBC Scotland, arrived. Autumn was turning swiftly into winter. I ditched the sports jacket and jeans for a down-packed duvet and ski pants and filled the motor with anti-freeze. The fans arrived at Firs Park in woolly jumpers and scarves. Les Thomson, mindful of the ground's lack of a proper drainage system, began praying for a mild winter. Postponements and rescheduled midweek fixtures would play havoc with his book-keeping.

Les had other problems, too. There had been mutterings among the players about the fact that Mr Bryan and his bus had to make a detour to pick up the chief executive at his home for every away match. Thomson's playing legacy was two dodgy knees and he didn't like walking, or driving, far. Newall had decided to play shop steward. On the day of the home match against East Fife, towards the middle of the month, the two men met in Thomson's office.

'Er, Les, the boys have been talking and they would prefer it if we didn't have to go out of our way to pick you up for away matches.'

'The players said that?'

'Aye.'

'The fucking players said that? I am not having my life run by fucking players.'

'Well, how's about if I pick you up before the match, run you to the ground, you can travel on the bus and then I'll run you home again?'

And so it was agreed. On away days, the club manager would be taxi driver to the club's chief executive.

Then we discovered we were without a physio. DJ's wife was about to give birth and he was away. As a joke, I let it be known that I held an ancient St John Ambulance first aid certificate, dating back around thirty years, and was a dab hand with the sponge. To my astonishment, they took the suggestion seriously. All sorts of nasty possibilities began to race through my mind: a home player could break a leg, suffer a heart attack onfield or even have a nervous break-down in the dressing room.

Above all, I imagined the reactions of the acerbic Shire support when I attempted to sprint out into the middle to tend a fallen player. The Dead End Kids, who barracked unmercifully everything set in front of them, would have a field day. Already they had clocked the down duvet; I was Michelin Man.

'I never brought any boots,' I said.

'We have plenty of spare boots,' said Jimmy Wilson, leering in anticipation.

'I've got a bad back.'

'Well, go and see the physio, he'll put you right.'

'There's no physio,' I replied triumphantly.

In the end, the East Fife physio agreed to double up.

The chairman was plainly irreversibly high on the smell of liniment and sweat and I arrived in the dressing room to find him again in the midst of the troops bellowing battle orders. He was in fine form.

When I walked in he was in galvanised discussion with The Cat, and performing an elaborate mime that involved an elbow in the face and a stamp on a foot. 'Look at the size of this c**t' he said admiringly of The Cat. The keeper preened himself and flexed his muscles. 'What's that boy's name?' he asked Dennis Newall of David Harvey, the ever-present full-back. Then, to Ross Donaldson: 'I like you. I wouldn't like to have played against you. You are an evil bastard.' Ross smiled his menacing smile of delight.

The game started badly. An error by Joe Robertson put the East Fife centre-forward clean through and he scored easily. Robertson cast a fearful eye at the Shire dugout. Dennis spat his derision, Greig Denham followed suit, the subs in the dugout joined in. It was like a baseball bullpen. The mud in front of us became speckled white with the stuff.

Eleven minutes before half-time Robertson planted a free-kick on the head of the Steven Oates to make it 1-1. A volley of spit flew out of the East Fife dugout next door. Joe had rescued himself from a bollocking and the Shire had remained unbeaten for two weeks. 'We're on a roll,' said the manager. Then, as an afterthought: 'In the league at any rate.'

The Scottish Cup first-round draw had given the Shire an away tie with Greenock Morton and we began to con-template another fall at the first hurdle of another cup competition. Dennis Newall thought 3-0, to them, would be a good result. Les Thomson's mind was on more practical matters. He had his accountant's hat on. Morton are the best-supported club outside the SPL and a gate of between 3,000 and 4,000 could be expected at Cappielow. A huge payday, in Shire terms, just for turning up – and losing. 'It should be worth a few bob to us,' said Les cheerfully.

The prospect loosened the purse strings and he called in Mr Bryan and his bus to bear seven of us – two Falkirk-based players, kitman Jimmy and his assistant Bobby, myself, Les

Thomson and Alex Forsyth – in stately splendour to Glasgow, where we were to pick up the manager, his assistant and the rest of the players. But the west of Scotland had been savaged by a cold snap on the Friday night and we had just reached the Glasgow Hilton, the rendezvous, when Les took the call on his mobile. Cappielow was frost-bound, the game was off. It was 1.30 p.m.

We decided to go in anyway. Les, his generosity by now out of control, ordered a round of coffees and blanched only mildly when he was handed a bill for £40. The Shire players commandeered a corner of the hotel bar, wallowing in this unexpected taste of luxury.

We had company. The place was full of famous faces, most of them in green tracksuits. Celtic were due to play an Old Firm match at Ibrox that afternoon and had stayed overnight, families and all. The Shire players looked at them like awestruck schoolboys. The Celtic players, scattered around the hotel's public rooms, stared back with that self-conscious, defensive manner that famous sportsmen adopt when out and about.

And they, too, seemed to have their cosy little cliques: the Englishmen, Chris Sutton and Alan Thompson, were on their own in the bar, perhaps wondering what a pint of Boddingtons used to taste like; Jos Valgaeren, a one-man Belgian clique, was just round the corner. I thought of asking Sutton and Thompson for an autograph on behalf of the ten-year-old, Celtic-daft son of my flat-mate, found the necessary courage, and dangled a Hilton napkin in front of them.

Sutton looked up disdainfully: 'I don't do autographs on match day,' he said. Thompson hurried out, looking slightly embarrassed. One of the Shire players, returning from the washroom, held the door open for Valgaeren. He brushed past without a word. We watched from the window as the football millionaires boarded their superbus for the half-mile journey to Ibrox.

Sporting pratfalls, however, do not seem to be confined to the Shire. The Celtic bus had travelled five yards when it ground to a halt. Manager Martin O'Neill appeared and, like a fussing mother hen, shooed his players down the steps and walked them round the block. I wondered if, like their famous huddle, this was some sort of time-honoured and mystical pre-match preparation, but the truth was far more prosaic. Their police motorcycle outrider had gone missing. We looked out the other window and spotted him at once. He was in the Hilton hotel flowerbed finishing a fag.

For every non-Celtic fan this story did have a happy ending. Thirty minutes later, at Ibrox, Valgaeren gave away a penalty for handball and Sutton and Thompson were sent off. *Schadenfreude*, I think they call it.

Three days later we were back at Cappielow. Les had agreed to play the postponed tie on the Tuesday night which brought the usual problems. It amounted to a mass boycott. The manager was in Dortmund on business. Steven Oates had mumps. Shaggy was sick, too, and Jamie McKay, a rabid Celtic fan, was in Barcelona for a Champions League tie. DJ's wife still hadn't given birth so we were, again, without a physio and then Gordon Parks, the usual conduit between players and management, got a call on his mobile from Joe Robertson. His train from Clydebank had broken down in a tunnel just outside Glasgow Central. So we were without our midfield general, and captain, too. 'Did you bring your boots, Jeff?' asked Greig Denham with what I now recognise as heavy sarcasm. Or at least, that's what I hope I recognised in his voice. It could have been desperation . . .

In the absence of Robertson, his fellow Weegie Johnny

Walker took the captain's armband and at once went into leadership hyperdrive. 'Who the fuck are Morton?' he demanded as he stepped off the bus at Cappielow.

Morton, founded in 1874, are, in fact, one of the oldest clubs in Britain. When the Shire came calling they stood third in Division Two and had caused a minor sensation two months earlier when they had beaten Gretna 1-0 at home in the CIS Cup, one of only four defeats the Raydale millionaires were to suffer all season.

Cappielow was an impressive sight, even on a November night, with one all-seater stand and another known as The Cowshed with seating at the front and terracing at the rear. The Wee Dublin End contained a number of incongruous white benches bolted on to it and was empty. Behind, and a reminder that Clydeside was once the biggest ship-building operation in the world, towered a huge crane. The ground also had four alert paramedics in green uniforms, a motorised stretcher, billiard table turf, pies with meat in them and a tractor mower that Jimmy Wilson eyed with envy.

Scott Livingstone, showing the consistency and skill that was to characterise his whole season, opened the scoring on eight minutes, 'The Ton' levelled five minutes later and with the scores at 1-1 and a potential upset on the cards, Greig Denham was faced with his first solo team talk. A half-time interval lasts fifteen minutes and I had always marvelled at Dennis Newall's ability to fill this with exhortation and criticism exactly to the moment when the referee would knock on the door and ask: 'Ready, lads?'

Greig did his best and gave an assured performance, but unlike the manager, tended to concentrate on what they were doing right rather than what they had done wrong. Not surprisingly, he ran out of things to say and there was an awkward five minutes during which the players stood around in silence, only occasionally stamping their studs into the concrete floor.

Given all this, and the fact that the squad had been almost wiped out like the Old Guard at Waterloo, a 3-1 defeat was a creditable result. The cup adventure, every cup adventure, was over. Now the Shire could concentrate on the league. But the promised land, second from bottom of the Third Division, still looked a million miles away.

Hampden Park must be the most difficult national stadium to find in the world. It hides away coyly in a corner of Cathcart on Glasgow's south side, there are no signs to guide you from the city and I had to ask directions from the archetypical soccer family, a dad and two kids, decked out in football scarves. 'Just follow the crowds,' said dad with a smile.

There were no crowds, of course. Like many other clubs in Scotland's lower divisions, Queen's Park's glory days had long gone. But they had managed to maintain an oddly eclectic support, ranging from a peer of the realm to the infamous Trombone Man, who was once banned from a ground for carrying a deadly weapon – or rather a deadly musical instrument.

Being an amateur club, Queen's Park had traditionally attracted fans from the strict Victorian social structure, Glasgow's lower middle class, and not much has changed since. The club's famous supporters included Lord MacFarlane, Bob Crampsey, the Memory Man of Scottish football, and Labour MSP Michael Watson. Crampsey had been born just round the corner from the ground and still lived nearby. Watson had just been accused of wilful fire-raising and was also hot news; his mug-shot beamed out of the Queen's Park programme. The club even had their own chaplain. God was a fan.

Hampden, or rather new Hampden, had been completed in 2002 at a cost of some £70m, following the Heysel and

Hillsborough tragedies. The cash had come from lottery grants, Sportscotland and private sponsors. The result was a completely oval, medium-sized stadium with undeniable charm and lavish facilities. These facilities included two electric scoreboards suspended underneath the roofs at each end. When I arrived these read, with uncanny prescience, Queen's Park 0 East Stirlingshire 0. I also noticed that the dugouts were six rows up on the South Stand. Dennis Newall, who was back on duty, would have to shout very loudly.

It took me half an hour to find the away dressing room. I passed changing rooms for the 'ball persons' and 'entertainers', doping control rooms, offices, TV interview areas and a 'match control meeting room', whatever that was.

I took a peek inside one door marked 'officials' to find twelve lockers, and their personal physiotherapy room. A separate room, possibly under-used, housed female officials. There were lifts everywhere and I wandered from floor to floor like a little boy lost in a maze. The place appeared to be empty, although I did pass the occasional Shire player, looking just as puzzled, travelling in the opposite direction.

Eventually I reached civilisation, a huge, modern cafeteria. Someone had thoughtfully provided TV sets in the serving areas so that on international days you could actually remain there, feast on a Hampden Steak Pie at £1.80 a go, and never miss a kick. I had been told that the best vantage points were the north or south stands, but of course when Queen's Park met the Shire you could sit pretty much anywhere you liked. A crowd of 457 spreads out pretty thinly in a stadium built to house 55,000.

Uniquely, a Queen's Park away fixture offers Third Division players – or whatever division Queen's Park are in at the time – the chance to play at the country's national stadium, to quarter the hallowed turf, to dash down channels whose white lines are painted by a computerised white line marker. To put it another way, the regular spectators at Hampden Park could watch Zinedine Zidane there one week and Ross Donaldson the next.

Ross, a bowel emptier of habit before any match, could also squat on his own personal toilet bowl, and maybe reflect that Zidane, too, had once been there. He could change in his own individual locker and have a hair-drier to himself.

On the park, the voices of player and management echoed round the vast and (virtually) empty stadium. The genteel support behind us sat in almost total silence. The game was appalling, goalless and without character. At half-time the tannoy blared Katie Melua singing *Closest Thing to Crazy*, which was a neat summation of the fare on display. Bored to distraction, I spent the second half counting the crowd and attempting to work out why Billy Stark, the opposing manager, would wear football boots when he was fifty yards away from the pitch in his south stand dugout. I decided it was an ex-player's force of habit.

Despite the result, and a rare clean sheet, Dennis Newall was in an unusually bad mood. He was annoyed, he said, because three points would have lifted his side off the foot of the table for the first time that season. I corrected him. The Shire had lost 5-0 to Peterhead in the first game of the season, but Albion Rovers had lost 6-0 to Gretna on the same day. Strictly speaking, we had then been off the bottom of Division Three for the first time in three seasons. Dennis didn't take too kindly to this and told me so in no uncertain terms.

I left, suitably chastened, and drove back to Edinburgh pondering all the while another statistic: the Shire had been unbeaten, in the league at any rate, for the whole of November. As Dennis often told me, recognition from his peers and the Scottish Football League sponsors was long overdue.

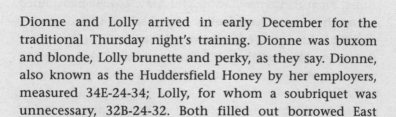

7

SEXY FOOTBALL

Dionne and Lolly arrived in early December for the traditional Thursday night's training. Dionne was buxom and blonde, Lolly brunette and perky, as they say. Dionne, also known as the Huddersfield Honey by her employers, measured 34E-24-34; Lolly, for whom a soubriquet was unnecessary, 32B-24-32. Both filled out borrowed East Stirlingshire FC jerseys and shorts rather nicely.

It had rained for much of the day and Firs Park was a quagmire. The wind sprints became laboured jogs after a couple of laps and to call the closing kick-about a bounce game was a laughable misnomer. The ball went splat and stuck. But that didn't dampen the girls' enthusiasm. They gamely ran round the park topless, rode piggy back atop a saucer-eyed Joe Robertson and Chris Baldwin, and then posed for photographs.

As the reporter/minder that turned up with them was later to put it: 'The game lads were more than happy to show their ball skills and have a kick around with our busty beauties.' Unfortunately for the lads, the busty beauties changed and showered in the away dressing room. You can't have everything.

The new signings were from *Sunday Sport*, the bottom-of-the-market tabloid that once revealed that scientists had found a London Transport bus on the moon and discovered the hide-and-seek world champion dead in a closet. Now the newspaper was in the fantasy land of East Stirlingshire FC. To *Sunday Sport*, the Shire's recent playing record was scarcely less believable than the woman in Bologna with sixty-two-inch breasts, or pet dogs that can recite the alphabet backwards. The visit of Lolly and Dionne was inevitable; the only mystery was why it took them so long.

The Shire were always going to be fodder for this sort of thing. *Front* magazine had led the way, *Loaded* had joined in and the only justification for Gordon Parks' weekly column in the *Daily Record* was that he was playing for Britain's worst football club. It simply wouldn't have worked at Stenhousemuir, or Cowdenbeath; they won games occasionally.

The Shire board had cottoned on to this, too, and after initial opposition from an outraged Alex Forsyth had decided to throw the gates open to any newspaper, magazine or radio station bent on scoffing sarcasm. Most, however, were taken aback when Les Thomson asked for payment. Les and the board had decided, in effect, to go into the business of marketing a dead loss.

Early in the New Year the *Scottish Sun*, or 'Your Soaraway' *Scottish Sun* as it likes to be called, joined the party. They would give Dennis Newall £100m, or at least a metaphorical £100m, and allow him to pick his Dream Team. He would become Jose Mourinho for a day.

It was a typical *Sun* scam involving their own unique mix of fact and fantasy and, having spent twelve months toiling as a sub-editor in the Dickensian squalor of the newspaper's old Kinning Park base, I can take an educated guess and work out how it all came to pass. A quiet news day, the Old Firm and their respective press offices in hibernation after Hogmanay, and the necessity to fill the paper with something. Some fevered furrowing of brows and scratching of heads and then the brainwave: 'I've got it, what if we give £100m to the manager of Scotland's worst team and see what he comes up with?' A quick consultation of the Third Division table and: 'Let's give it to East Stirlingshire. Who's their manager again?'

Dennis Newall's reaction when they got in touch was instantaneous: 'Cash or a cheque?' he asked. But he sportingly pitched in and chose a Shire side that include Gianluigi Buffon in goal, John Terry in defence and Thierry Henry up front. To the delight of the *Scottish Sun*, he went £26m over budget and was forced to put three of his own players on the bench. Quite wisely, he refused to name them. 'I don't want them to think they've arrived,' he said. 'I don't want that going to their heads.'

The visit from Lolly and Dionne certainly seemed to have gone to some heads and Firs Park was becoming like a nudist beach. Male folk from Glasgow do seem to have an exhibitionist nature. I once conducted an hour-long interview with the seventy-year-old former convenor of the Scottish Communist Party in his Bishopbriggs home and he sat throughout stripped to the waist. His wife told me this was quite usual and that he often received visitors clad only in his underpants.

At Firs Park, this sort of carry-on was almost the norm. The Shire's little sweeper, Johnny Walker, liked to listen to the manager's pre-match team talk, and his post-match inquest, totally naked. Even the award of the captaincy had no effect on this distressing routine. When Gordon Parks, who had collected £20 off every player for the Christmas party, failed to show with the kitty, his punishment was to do a lap of Firs Park totally naked and then take a penalty against Ross Gilpin. Not surprisingly, the keeper took his eye off the ball and Parks, to the astonishment of the watchers from the windows on Firs Street, then did a gruesome lap of honour. A season with the Shire, for all its accumulated miseries, did have its lighter moments.

'The only way is up,' Lolly had twittered to the love-smitten boys at Firs Park by way of farewell. She, and they, probably had something else in mind, but in terms of the remainder of the season she had it about right.

By December, and the arrival of second-bottom Albion Rovers at Firs Park, there was still plenty to play for; still, as managers like to say, a long way to go. Gretna and Peterhead had run away with the promotion places in Division Three, but the second half of the season was far from meaningless for the also-rans. Players were performing for the right to earn continued employment as professional footballers, managers for the right to hang on to their jobs. In the case of the Shire, the Holy Grail was the right to be known henceforth as the second-worst side in British football. That title was currently held by Albion Rovers. This was a crunch game in every respect. How apt then that the manager of the Wee Rovers, as distinct from their much larger neighbours Raith Rovers, was known as Crunchie McAllister.

Kevin McAllister had joined the club in December 2003 after a playing career that included a spell at Chelsea. Around 5 foot 3 inches tall and with a pinched, cheeky chappie Scottish face, he strode up and down the technical area dressed in a black leather coat over a sports jacket. A pair of black leather gloves completed the ensemble. He looked like a Glasgow debt collector.

'For fuck's sake gi' us something, ref,' he would bawl at the referee at frequent intervals until the official, a magisterial, grey-haired figure some 6 foot 5 inches tall, lost patience and walked over to confront his tiny tormentor at the halfway line. 'Aye, I'll gi' you something, Crunchie,' he said. 'I'll gi' you the opportunity to sit in the stand if you don't pipe down.' McAllister, looking like a chastened schoolboy, returned to the dugout cackling at this rare example of official wit.

Despite November's unbeaten league run, Newall was still convinced that his job was on the line. 'Mackin wouldn't hesitate,' he said. 'Those fuckers out there [his players] could lose me my job. Bobby Robson, Paul Sturrock, they've all been casualties. Rowan Alexander [the Gretna manager], if he loses another couple of games the jury will be out on him big time. He's even easier to replace than me.

'Managers used to be ten a penny, now they're 100 a penny. Just replace them, that's the easy answer nowadays. Then they say the manager's lost the dressing room. That's ridiculous, crap. All it means is that the directors don't have the man-management to manage their manager. East Stirling are in my heart now. I can't try and blame the last manager. I have to do it myself. But sometimes I wonder why some of these guys signed on here.

'The worst thing is I can't do anything about it after three o'clock. I can't go out and play for them. My life is in their hands.'

The players seemed to have got that message. They had become more assertive, more gung-ho. The things they were going to do to the Wee Rovers were indescribable. 'Kill the bastards,' roared The Cat. 'Get right up their noses,' offered Johnny Walker. Even the new boy had a go. 'Win the battle,' piped up Iain Diack quietly, and a little self-consciously, as he laced up his boots.

Diack had arrived on loan the week previously from the Shire's Scottish Cup conquerors Greenock Morton. A full-time footballer alleged to be making £200 a week, he lived on a new-build estate in Cumbernauld, surrounded, it was said, by adoring neighbours basking in the reflected glow of celebrity. Diack, in a downmarket way, was to Cumbernauld what an Old Firm player was to Helensburgh: a little bit of glamour in suburban Glasgow.

But Diack was assuredly old Cumbernauld, a throwback to an era where even the police dogs walked the town's streets in threes. He proudly informed Dennis Newall that he has just bought a pit bull terrier. Dennis's jaw dropped. He did a double-take.

'Hang on, Iain, haven't you got an eighteen-month-old daughter?'

'Aye, so?'

'And hasn't your wife got another on the way?'

'Aye, so what?'

'Iain, you see that big white bone your dog was chewing in the kitchen . . .?'

Diack seemed to have taken that awful thought into the game with him. Against Albion Rovers, his first touch of the ball was greeted by a low mooing from the direction of the thirty-strong travelling support huddled together in the corrugated shed opposite. This was a sure sign that he was one of their ex-players and he seemed to take the barracking to heart. His game went downhill from there. The Shire were just as bad and after one ludicrous gaffe I caught the Rovers bench breaking one of the unwritten rules at this level of football and laughing out loud at the incompetence of the opposition.

With the Shire a goal down at half-time, Dennis went to war. He was all silver-tongued eloquence and inspiration. 'Cat, your kicking's shite.' Not that that really needed pointing out. 'Ross, you must have spent the night in fucking Burger King.' Getting back to normal.

I looked around to see the Norwegian midfielder blanching at the level of invective. Before he arrived in Scotland he had never heard the f-word, let alone the c-word. He had told me earlier he was slowly getting used to it, but his education was just beginning. Having disposed of the rest of the midfield in his inimitable way, Dennis Newall turned to Shaggy and asked: 'Were you shagging that big burd last night, or something?' Shaggy winced in pain, his teammates chortled.

Newall wasn't finished and warmed to his task. 'This lot,' he said, gesturing at the wall that divided the home and away dressing rooms, 'are the worst bunch of shite I have seen all season. They are the biggest bunch of shite in Division Three and that's saying something. We should be murdering them, murdering them.' His words had their effect. The Shire began to murder them. Early in the second half, Diack was held back in the box and Joe Robertson scored the equalising penalty.

The draw left the Wee Rovers a tantalising three points ahead in the table and within a week was to offer support to another pet theory of mine: Dennis Newall had the safest job in Scottish football; many rival managers, on the other hand, must have woken in a cold sweat in the middle of the night before a Shire fixture, imagining their fate if the unthinkable happened and they lost. Or even drew. Sure enough, within a couple of weeks, Crunchie and his leather coat were given their marching orders.

You lose some, you win some. Dennis did get his reward for November's efforts when the Bell's Third Division Manager of the Month award arrived – in a cardboard box. In the absence of a representative from Bell's or the Scottish Football League, the manager had to present it to himself for the benefit of the photographer from the *Falkirk Herald*.

But at least the thought was there and Newall was genuinely delighted. He put it rather nicely when he said: 'My name is on this trophy, but it belongs to everyone. I get the bullets when they are flying and the plaudits when things start to go well but it is reward for all involved at East Stirlingshire.' Technically speaking, it was the club's first silverware since the Stirlingshire Cup of 2000 and would have helped fill out the boardroom trophy cabinet. Dennis, however, decided to take his award home with him.

With winter biting deep, and postponements – of both fixtures and training nights – beginning to mount, the players began to get as rusty as the Shire's ancient silverware. Christmas, along with girlfriends, the traditional anathema to football managers who do not like the prospect of idle, bloated – or sated – playing staff, was looming. The problem now was getting another game.

Livingston stepped into the breach by agreeing to a friendly on the eleventh, with Jimmy Wilson and Bobby Jack – in the absence of volunteers – acting as ball boys. The trip to Montrose a week later was called off in the early morning. The Shire fans, who had already set off to Montrose before the postponement, drowned their sorrows in the Nelson, the Anchor, the Caledonian, and Sharkies.

But the away game at Peterhead the day after Boxing Day went ahead, with the Shire suffering the traditional seasonal hangover and losing 3-0. Once again, Martin Bavidge, the ginger bogeyman of the Shire, was on the score sheet, tucking away the third. All three goals were headers, again putting a question mark over the lack of height and spring in the Shire defence. 'I'd give anything for a basketball player,' said Newall. 'Even a small basketball player.'

A new year was dawning. But not a new dawn. It opened

with old Scottish weather. A howling gale was battering Firs Park, whipping old plastic cups and fag ends up into the air around the ground as I arrived for the Stenhousemuir match on New Year's Day. All the players – remarkably a full complement and even more remarkably looking stone-cold sober, not a pink eye or a ruby lip in sight – were seated round the dressing room, wearing their suits.

As always, most of them were leafing through the matchday programme to see if they had earned a mention, or even a picture. Ross Donaldson didn't bother. His picture, the same picture of him in action in the second match of the season against Gretna, was on the front of every programme throughout the season. The Littlewoods budget, apparently, would not run to a change of cover.

The thought of fans paying £1.50 to see Ross Donaldson in glorious Technicolor was another of the manager's pet bugbears. 'You see that fat c**t, he'll be showing it to his mates in the pub,' said Dennis. 'It'll go to his head. He'll think he's arrived. They all think they've arrived.'

The manager muttered on and on about his legacy. Greig Denham joined in occasionally. The general consensus was that, given the opportunity, they would bin the lot. In the distance, a phone could be heard ringing constantly in Les Thomson's office up the corridor. I noticed a single Christmas card on the filing cabinet. The players must have sent their seasonal greetings to the manager's home address.

The howling gale had brought a serious selection problem. The Cat couldn't kick a dead ball any distance at the best of times. In these conditions he might not get it out of his own area. Dennis called the keeper into the office to give him the bad news. 'You're dropped. You can't kick in that gale so Ross Gilpin will start.'

The Cat, who had made a string of fine saves at Peterhead,

was distraught. He howled his frustration: 'Gaffer, I've done nothing wrong. Gi' us a break. I played all right last week and I've been working on my line-kicks, you'll see.'

'I'm not arguing, now fuck off,' Newall told him.

Fifteen minutes later The Cat's pride and dignity were restored when the game was postponed. We had a day off.

The January transfer window arrived and three new faces appeared. The recruits, or potential recruits as they still had to prove themselves, had to strip and shower in the referee's quarters, it being an unbreakable rule of football that only players signed for the club can change in the first-team room.

One of the new faces possessed what in Scottish football circles could be considered a 'name'; Derek Rae had begun his career with Glasgow Rangers where his brother, Alex, was performing with some distinction. This was perhaps another example of what Shire fans regard as the famous brother syndrome. Martin Ferguson had followed Alex as manager; the brother of Gordon Durie, of Rangers and Scotland fame, had also been in the Shire hot-seat. Now we had Derek Rae.

'They told me I could sign Rae and I signed the wrong one,' said Dennis. Greig Denham added, mysteriously: 'It's getting like a young offenders' institute at Firs Park now. A lot of baggage.' At first, I assumed he meant Daft Dougie, the deputy assistant groundsman from the borstal up the road. But Daft Dougie had gone by then. Two prison officers had arrived one morning a month earlier to cart him off, protesting, to some unknown destination. Jimmy and Bobby had been left to plod on in lonely tandem.

The baggage Denham referred to was therefore, presumably, being carried around by some of the players now seated in the home dressing room. Johnny Walker, one of the few

Shire players admired by the management, if only for his combative streak and dislike of losing, had been sacked by Hamilton Academicals the previous year after failing a drugs test. He later admitted taking cocaine at a party.

Joe Robertson, like Walker, was a diminutive Glaswegian and like many diminutive Glaswegians he instilled an unsettling feeling that you wouldn't like to get on the wrong side of him. Once when he was wrestling playfully with David Harvey in the dressing room I had urged him, jokingly, to 'pick on someone his own size.' 'It doesn't matter what size they come to me,' he said meaningfully, looking me up and down.

Joe regularly missed training or matches, always with the same excuse that: 'ScotRail had fucked up again'. Gordon Parks, his best pal, had another theory – Joe's 'trouble and strife'. It was a surprise to me that the player, an out-of-work taxi driver who had also worked occasionally as a labourer, turned up at all. The club gave him £6 a week to travel from Clydebank to Falkirk three times a week and I defy anyone to manage that without either walking all the way, or hitch-hiking. The joke in the dressing room was that the only way he could get round it was by doing a Billy Connolly and hiding in the lavvy when the ticket man came.

Whenever he missed training Dennis, sticking to the rule he had for everyone, automatically dropped him, and this he could ill-afford to do. Robertson was an accomplished player with a fierce will to win, could score goals and was streetwise beyond belief. He had been around, as they say. He would regularly win two or three free-kicks a match in potential goal-scoring positions, not by diving, but by folding his knee as he was tackled, and contorting his face with a convincing wince. The referee bought it every time.

But still he was dropped. 'There's that wee ned living in

some high-rise in Clydebank and here's me ringing him at Christmas with a Grand Marnier in one hand and a cigar in the other, I felt really bad about that,' said Dennis Newall without, it must be said, much conviction.

As for Derek Rae, he offered another answer to the questions that had been plaguing me since the start of the season: why would twenty or so nominally sane young men subject themselves to the thrice-weekly humiliation that went with being a registered player with East Stirlingshire FC? Why suffer beastings in training, ritual disembowelment every Saturday, slagging-offs from mates at work or in the pub and toe-curling invective from the coaching staff for a tenner a week?

Playing staff apart, why would Jimmy Wilson and Bobby Jack devote almost three decades of their lives apiece to this raddled institution for a pittance, in the case of Jimmy, and for no feasible reward in the case of Bobby? On training nights both dipped into their own pockets for bread and soup for the players and never attempted to claim anything back.

And why, given that the club's fans had long ago rationalised the traditional tenet of football support – the celebration of victory – into a smiling acceptance of the inevitable, would they turn up week after week? Most of the players, of course, wanted to be involved in senior football, to be able to put 'Professional Footballer' alongside occupation on mortgage application forms. Or, and more likely as most of them were single, employ their status as a chat-up line.

But Rae offered another justification. He had been playing for Hednesford Town in the Vauxhall Conference. He was thirty years old, unfit, and like many Scottish footballers at Third Division level was at what Dennis Newall would describe as 'the arse-end' of his career. And he had baggage. He had given up alcohol in 1999, following the example of his older brother, and like many reformed drinkers viewed the world through the wary eyes of a man half expecting a pint of Tennents to creep up behind and mug him.

He had cause enough to lapse. Unlike his brother, he did not possess the footballing talent to salvage a worthwhile career and at Christmas he had lost his job and his mortgage. His fiancée was expecting a baby.

For one away game, with his first-born due at any moment, Rae still climbed on to the team bus for the long trip to Montrose. He was a substitute, the Shire lost 4-1 and he did not get any playing time. On the way home he got the call: Natalie was in labour. He missed the birth of his daughter by fifteen minutes, but he was still back training a week later. Perhaps playing for the Shire was a form of redemption. From there, the only way was up; one match day, or training day, at a time.

On 8 January, we made the return trip to Kate Adie Land in conditions so bad that even the stock car racers had given up. The cold was mind-numbing, a vicious wind blew down Central Park and black clouds in the direction of the Forth Road Bridge turned day into night. It looked like the end of the world.

I had on a duvet, long johns under the ski pants, a scarf and a woolly hat and still felt perished. After twenty minutes in the dugout Greig Denham was going down with hypothermia and I had to lend him a spare hat. The Cat had to be thawed out with a pummelling from DJ in the dressing room at half-time. Tad told me, smugly, that the Cowdenbeath press box had a heater, but I noted, (smugly), that as the game wore on the condensation on the windows made it impossible to see any action.

Not that there was much to see for a Shire follower and it was a black day for the manager in particular. His son, Chris, had recently jumped ship to Cowdenbeath – for £100 a week – and although dad inevitably had his foot in both camps there was little doubt that he wanted the family bragging rights. He had warned Chris on the phone the night before about the probability of wind-ups from his former team-mates. His debut had been against Gretna and the Blue Brasil had lost 8-0. 'Don't, whatever you do, get sent off,' warned Dennis.

Cowdenbeath took an early lead, but Jamie McKay's header and a Joe Robertson effort gave the Shire a 2-1 advantage at the interval. But they lost Johnny Walker through a leg injury just before half-time and Chris Baldwin – Dennis's target for abuse for the day in the absence of Paul Ross – had to play on after suffering a cut finger, an act of heroism he underlined by showing us all the offending digit at half-time and throwing in a few convincing winces and grimaces.

The home side had the advantage of the howling gale in the second half and swiftly perfected a tactical master plan – they would simply give away a succession of goal-kicks and then latch on to The Cat's feeble attempts to get the ball up the park. To Cat's acute embarrassment, Jamie McKay had to take over the goal-kicking in the end. But not before the home centre forward had completed his hat-trick. A 2-1 lead had dissolved into a 3-2 defeat.

It may have been the heightened expectation after a few good results, or simply that he had wanted to get one over on his son, but the manager's post-match tirade was brutal: 'You pressed the fucking self-destruct button again,' he began. 'We are not miracle workers. You see some of youse? You couldn't get a game with a fucking amateur team now. Shaggy, twice on the ball, you delivered it to someone of theirs. You have got to commit yourselves. There was not one decent ball through to the forwards.

'See you, Chris Baldwin; you need to build yourself up. You are just not strong enough on the fucking ball. Today we were playing against men, MEN, who know the importance of winning. Some of youse will be saying we are wrong. We are not fucking wrong. We are fucking right. See in this game? You don't get caught square, you don't get caught with long balls over the head. See today, we were up against the biggest bag of shite I have seen in senior football and we made them look half decent because we couldn't pass, we couldn't tackle, we couldn't fucking time the jumps.

'Every fucking department was weak today. Weak. It was weak when we got here and it's still weak. There is an acceptance here that we are shite. How many's left since we arrived? I tell you what, there will be more. There is no safety net here because where do you go from here? I will tell you – you go down the fucking toilet.'

His mood had changed little by Monday's training night. Derek Ure, the top scorer the previous season and a local Falkirk boy, had watched as Iain Diack came in to take the first-choice striking place. Against Cowdenbeath, Ure hadn't even managed a place on the bench. But he could have chosen a better time to ask for a free transfer.

Dennis knew what was coming as Ure had told Les Thomson and Les had warned Dennis. In the dressing room Ure was in early as usual, visibly preparing himself for the confrontation ahead. 'You go in there and give him hell,' said Bobby Jack, a big Derek Ure fan and a friend of the family. The meeting was over in thirty seconds flat. 'Gaffer, I want a move. I used to love coming down here. I don't get a first team chance. I want a free transfer,' announced Ure. And the gaffer replied: 'Del, you are going nowhere.

Now get the fuck out of here.' And that was that. 'I have never seen so many petted lips at any one club,' said Greig Denham.

I had noticed a subtle change in Dennis, and Greig for that matter, since the Manager of the Month award. He was definitely more confident, more assertive. He spent less and less time worrying about whether Mackin would bump him. His man-management could not be faulted. Having deflated Derek Ure, he at once decided to start him in the next match 'because he'll be sick as a dog and want to prove something to me'. When I left training that night he was tutoring an attentive-looking Cat in goalkicking, the ball landing with a splat on the sodden turf. As it turned out, The Cat's days were numbered. As were those of his fellow goal tender, Ross Gilpin.

Thanks to the strenuous efforts of the manager and his mobile phone, the fresh blood was pouring into Firs Park, most of it of surprisingly rich quality. A new goalkeeper, two midfielders and a defender. The new No. 1 was Derek Jackson, a thirty-nine-year-old prison officer who worked at Glen Ochil. A custodian in every sense of the word. He had spent almost a decade at Arbroath before work commitments forced him out of the professional game. He had a spell with Sauchie Juniors, now he was back in 'the big time' as he smilingly called it.

For what turned out to be an epic victory over Queen's Park at the end of January, Dennis had also thrown that ubiquitous player of football everywhere, A. Trialist, in at the deep end. A. Trialist turned out to be a blond, former SPL player (who, amazingly, wasn't even in his forties and past the 'arse-end' of his career) and one-time Scotland Under-21 internationalist called Chris McGroarty. He played a blinder. So did Jackson.

Alongside McGroarty, midfielder Paul Tyrell also made his debut. His brother Mark was to arrive not long afterwards. The Tyrells were known as Bucket and Spade. Both turned up for every match in matching pinstripe suits, but they could not have been further apart in looks and playing styles. Paul, balding and built like a weightlifter, churned on massive legs through mud and opposition alike; he was the Jonah Lomu of the Scottish Third Division. The Dead End Kids immediately christened him The Tank. Mark had a more delicate touch, but had pace and could tackle.

The Queen's Park match was Shire's first since 15 January when Elgin City had won at Firs Park and 'got the Shire monkey off our backs', as their manager put it later. Ross Gilpin had one of his best games in goal, but still let in three. The defeat by Elgin prompted Dennis Newall to apologise to McGroarty in front of his potential new team-mates for 'the fucking shambles you've landed in. I apologise for bringing you here, son.'

Greig Denham, too, offered more evidence that he was maturing into management with the most damning speech I had ever heard from him. The good cop days were forgotten when he came out with: 'Willie Martin, you made him look like a superstar today. Willie Martin! Who the fuck is he? There is no fucking hunger. None of you are willing to take a body, give it them and say "how do you fucking like that?" You just lied down and gave in to that shite next door.

'We will do it, we will get there somehow. But nine goals in three games against us, it's worse than garbage. Defenders start well, then they lose concentration and it spreads everywhere. Every fucking where.'

It was a day for penance, as it turned out, with a steady stream of Shire players making their way to the manager's office. The defensive partnership of Jamie McKay and Stephen

Oates arrived one after the other, both embarrassingly contrite. Dennis was less than forgiving: 'Aye well,' he told each of them after their apologies. 'Get the fuck out of here – and do better next time.'

All was forgiven and forgotten against Queen's Park. There was a tangible feeling that the day might produce something special, with bright sunshine bathing Firs Park and the sight of McGroarty lining up again. There had been talk of him going to Lincoln City in the English Third Division or Cowdenbeath, who also seemed to possess the means to pay players far more than the Shire would, or could.

Jackson oozed confidence and Paul Tyrell wore a fierce, competitive mask. He was to tear the Queen's midfield to shreds. Up front, Derek Ure was back and eager, his starting place assured after the imminent departure of Iain 'Pitbull' Diack, who had been snapped up by Arbroath. Joe Robertson had missed his train again.

I actually missed the Shire's first goal since 8 January, scored by McGroarty, as I had been called into the chief executive's office. It was a moment of crisis. Les Thomson was busy counting the gate receipts and doing the wages. A pile of brown envelopes lay on the table in front of him. DJ the Physio had a theory as to why the players were paid in one pound coins: 'Les presses them himself in his office.' And there was, in truth, an awful lot of small change about . . .

I could tell right away the chief executive was not a happy man. He looked up from placing another pound coin into a brown envelope and asked: 'The title of this book, it's called *No Point*, isn't it? I hope you're not going to bring the good name of this club into disrepute.'

Until then I'd parried all questions regarding the book's title from management, players and the board, reasoning that they might not be too happy about being connected with something called *Pointless*. But now I was bang to rights. Apparently, some bright-young-thing from a local book shop had phoned in a state of high excitement to tell Thomson the good news and to ask if the chief executive and his players would be available for promotion work.

'No, that is not the title,' I answered quite truthfully, amid visions of being escorted out the aluminium door or, worse, having to face Mackin.

'What is it called then?'

'It's called *Pointless*. But that's only a working title. You are obviously not pointless now.'

'Well, that's not very nice. The board might not like that at all. It doesn't show us in a very good light. We've managed eight points already this season – it's not exactly all doom and gloom, you know.'

I was rescued midway between doom and gloom when a muffled roar from outside signalled a goal. 'There you go,' said Thomson in the resigned tones of a man who had heard such roars before. 'We're one down. I can always tell by the noise.'

But he had got it wrong this time. The noise had, in fact, signalled a Shire goal and I arrived back at the dugout to find the manager chewing on a celebratory, and illegal, Hamlet (it transpired he had seen the new Partick Thistle manager, Dick Campbell, puffing away in the dugout live on TV and took this as a FIFA sanction-busting precedent). The Queen's manager, Billy Stark – who had forsaken his football boots for the untested combination of a pair of brown brogues to go with his tracksuit (not a look that works for everyone) – was banging his head on the roof of the away dugout. From then on, the game unfolded into something akin to hysteria.

McGroarty scored his second, Shire player-coach Greig Denham then went down like a felled steer after a butt from the Queen's striker Ally Graham, before Graham himself pulled one back to make it 1-2. Our new keeper, as I had predicted to a disbelieving Shire bench, saved a penalty and then Diack signed off his illustrious, three-match Shire career by going down in the Queen's box, winning a penalty, and converting it himself.

There were scuffles, goal-line clearances, yellow cards and an electric moment when a Queen's Park central defender booted a spare ball deliberately, and with studied venom, into the main stand, almost decapitating Alex Forsyth. Only reflexes sharpened by his twice weekly line-dancing sessions saved him.

'I was only coming here for the bonus, you know,' said the new cult hero Derek Jackson. The displaced Cat did his best to smile. Most of the £50 home bonuses were spent in Falkirk's Sportmans Bar, alongside some of the Queen's Park players determined to get something out of the day. Ally Graham came down the corridor to the players' lounge to ask Greig Denham if he 'fancied a pint'. Greig, however, resisted the offer to smoke the pipe of peace over a lager. There was history there.

Greig used to polish Graham's boots when they were both on the books of Motherwell and, like the Joe Pesci character in *GoodFellas*, has never been allowed to forget it. Or allowed himself to forget it. Greig might have said: 'No more shoeshine, Ally.' Instead, he said: 'He can go fuck himself.'

WALKING IN A WINTER BLUNDERLAND

The blinding revelation struck as I was searching for a parking space close by the Sheriff's Court next to Albion Rovers' Cliftonhill ground. I had arrived just in time to see Jimmy Wilson and Bobby Jack wheeling Shire kit bags across the A89, dodging and weaving through the unyielding, Saturday afternoon, Asda-bound traffic. As ever, they had travelled in their own cars, paid their own petrol and were once again demonstrating their unfathomable devotion to the Shire; two middle-aged men, late middle-aged men, who should have known better, toiling for what everyone else on the planet would recognise at once as a lost cause. I realised, suddenly, that I had become very fond of them; all at once I loved this ramshackle football club: its earnest, hopeless players; its fanciful, battered fans; and its persistent, resilient management. My Damascene moment had arrived on the road to Coatbridge.

I confess here and now that I began the season with the hope – kept well concealed, of course – that the Shire would lose every match, farcically lose every match, and thus justify the title of the book. I had chortled inwardly at some of their errors and mocked them behind their backs to friends in the pub. When they did score in those early days, the smile I offered to the dugout and dressing room was stretched tight over gritted teeth.

By mid-February that had changed. I had come to realise that I wanted the Shire to win. From my privileged position in the dugout I now lived every tackle, every pass, and every shot at goal. I was mortified by their near-misses, railed at opposing players and spat and cursed and paced in the dugout alongside the manager. I high-fived him after the rare goals for, nodded earnestly at his tactical discourses and bounced his opinions right back at him. 'That No. 11 of theirs is killing us,' he would say. 'He's killing us, that No. 11,' I would reply. I was Phil Neal to his Graham Taylor, a gormless, mobile listening post into which he could pour his frustrations, bias and outbreaks of tactical nous.

My involvement was almost physical. At Firs Park the previous week I had abused the linesman to such an extent that he had threatened to have me banished to the stand. In the dressing room at half-time I had nodded my appreciation when the manager praised, and looked away when he bawled. I had shaken hands with the players and wished them luck before the match; I had consoled them after it. I caught myself, in one pub conversation, referring to them as 'we'. Unrestricted access to the Shire had transformed me from cynical chronicler into rabid fan.

At the Cliftonhill players' entrance came more evidence of this unlikely conversion. I was greeted by an elderly gateman, shuffling and shivering in the biting cold, and three sniggering accomplices. All were dressed in the colours of the home team, gateman included.

'Can I help you?'

'I'm with the Shire.'

'Aye, he has to be with them, he's wearing specs.'

'That Ross Donaldson, he's an arse.'

'I beg your pardon?'

'That Ross Donaldson. An arse.'

'Excuse me, but do you know Ross Donaldson?'

'Nah, but I've seen him play.'

'But how do you know he's an arse?'

'He just looks it.'

'Well you look like an arse. And you. And you. And you.'

The four of them looked at me meaningfully. This was Coatbridge after all. 'You see that up there,' said the gateman. I looked up to a sign that read 'Welcome to Cliftonhill'. 'If you carry on like that then that will no longer apply. Now in you go. Do you want a programme, by the way?'

'You should have dobbed him,' said Jimmy Wilson, but by then the ludicrousness of the situation had sunk in. I had risked a hammering on behalf of a Bellshill van driver/footballer over absolutely nothing. I had been pre- pared to take on three other middle-aged men for the honour of a football club to which I felt no fealty whatsoever. Jimmy smiled, looked at Bobby, raised his eyebrows and smiled again: 'He's caught it, hasn't he, Bobby?'

'Aye, son,' said Bobby. 'You've got the Shire-itis. God help you now.'

True to form, the single Cliftonhill toilet did not run to any paper and Ross Donaldson, unaware that I had just come close to laying down my life for him, ordered me next door to 'nick some off the ref'. 'That's a job that suits you,' he added unnecessarily.

The arrival of the super-soft toilet roll and Ross's move into the little room in the corner was the signal for a mass exodus and we moved swiftly outside to be greeted by the usual torrent of bile from the Cliftonhill fans gathered above and around the tunnel.

On a grassy knoll close by a block of council flats on the far side of the ground a four-wheel-drive vehicle, possibly a

Freeloader, had been parked precariously while its contents – two young children, boy and girl, father/driver and an elderly man on a stick – flung abuse from afar at the Shire.

This was the final meeting with Albion Rovers and seemed likely to decide the Third Division wooden spoon. Crunchie, of course, had gone, and had been replaced by the former Motherwell player, Jimmy Lindsay, and under him Rovers had managed to steady the ship. Their lead over the Shire, at the bottom, had been stretched to four points. But there wasn't much passion in a game of such dubious import and midway though the first half my mind began to wander. The occupants of the four-wheel drive had given up shouting and even the home support had fallen silent. Dennis Newall and Greig Denham had been rendered almost mute by the quality of the fare before them.

On the pitch, the Shire did take the lead early in the second half when Donaldson played in Steven Oates, but within two minutes the Wee Rovers had levelled. Then all hell broke loose. One of the Albion players slid in brutally on Paul Ross and the Shire piled in *en masse*. Johnny Walker, coming from Glasgow, naturally picked on the biggest Rovers player. Joe Robertson, also coming from Glasgow, jumped off the bench and began to harangue the linesman. Ross Donaldson, being Ross Donaldson, landed a love tap on the nearest Rovers man.

To me, it was evidence that the Shire were a team at last; they were willing to go to war for each other. But it had to be said the fight was far more entertaining that the football. The referee, too, seemed to sense this as the yellow cards remained in his breast pocket and although his linesman urged him to take action against Ross 'Iron Mike' Donaldson, the Shire's heavyweight pugilist got away with a gentle telling-off. 'I told you he was an arse,' said the gateman on the way out.

A week later, ahead of the home match against Montrose, it was announced that we had lost Gordon Parks and the source of most of the dressing room wit and occasional wisdom. The striker had been 'suspended' by chairman Mackin, apparently because the *Daily Record* had reneged on a deal which allowed him to write his weekly diary on the Shire. The *Record* had refused to cough up after Littlewoods had moved in with their 'six-figure' sponsorship and Mackin, in his Paisley way, was simply extracting revenge.

Parksy, it must be said, had sailed pretty close to the wind with his Monday morning Shire soap opera. His remarks about the fat referee at New Bayview had seen him hauled before the Hampden beaks and his revelations about training conditions at Firs Park had not gone down well with the board.

Dennis Newall was seriously concerned. The player's fifteen-year career had given him a lot of contracts which the manager was happy to use. Parks was also the main reason that Joe Robertson and Johnny Walker were playing for a tenner a week when they could plainly find more meaningful employment elsewhere. Within a couple of days of the banishment Robertson announced that he would not be coming back.

The long hand of Mackin was everywhere. Goalkeeper Ross Gilpin, made virtually redundant by the arrival of Derek Jackson had, as twenty year olds tend to, complained to his dad. Dad had complained to Mackin and, at the chairman's suggestion, had then phoned Dennis Newall. 'What did you say to him?' I asked the manager. 'I told him to fuck off.' So that was the end of Ross Gilpin, and his dad.

Montrose had arrived on the back of a poor run of ten games without a win and, urged on by a tall, tracksuited figure with a stentorian Cockney voice who turned out to be the son of the former Dundee and Spurs legend Alan Gilzean, they scored first with a soft penalty and led 1-0 at half-time.

Dennis's dressing room targets were predictable: Ross Donaldson must up his work-rate, Derek Ure must find his shooting boots and Jamie McKay, who gave away the penalty, was a fat c∗∗t and an unfit fat c∗∗t at that. Why settle for one insult when there is room for two, seemed to be Dennis's motto.

The weather was appalling, the pitch an almost unplayable morass. 'They [Montrose] will moan about it if they lose or draw,' forecast Jimmy Wilson. But they didn't lose or draw. Ure did eventually find his shooting boots but Montrose, as if on some hidden cue, snatched the winner in the ninetieth minute. There were no complaints about the pitch.

Dennis's blazing post mortem was conducted to a backdrop of triumphant war whoops from next door and afterwards he was as low as I had ever seen him. As ever in circumstances like this, fate continued to put the boot in.

Sean McAuley, another of the old guard who had been marginalised when the new management team arrived, marched into Newall's office, muddy football boots under his arm, and announced he was quitting. The manager needed him badly but McAuley was adamant. He would, he insisted, not only never play for the Shire again, but also would never play football again. Greig Denham shouldered the press out of the way as he was leaving. 'Oh dear, oh dear,' said Les Thomson.

But, a week later, at least Parksy was back, his suspension suspended, at least for the time being. According to him, he was the only reason that Chris McGroarty had turned down £150 a week from Cowdenbeath to stay and earn £10 a week with the Shire. Dennis Newall claimed it was his own man-management skills. 'It doesn't say much about their manager's powers of persuasion,' he mused, perhaps forgetting that that manager had succeeded in tempting his own son to the club.

Robertson had gone for good and in common with most managers in the depths of winter Newall had to contemplate a lengthy injury list before the trip to Stenhousemuir. There were, however, two new faces: a Slovakian who didn't speak any English and who Dennis claimed he had flown in by easyJet, and Mark Tyrell, brother of Paul.

The Stenhousemuir danger man, as always, was Paul McGrillen, a former team-mate of Greig Denham at Motherwell. McGrillen scored the first goal and went on to make it a hat-trick. Most of Dennis's wrath was directed at the hapless Paul Ross, who was playing as an emergency full-back. Jimmy Lindsay in the Stenhousemuir dugout had cottoned on to this at once and had started to direct all the traffic down Ross's channel. Ross hadn't a clue about defending but, to be fair, as a midfielder he shouldn't have had a clue about defending. But that didn't stop Newall. 'Squeeze up, Paul.' 'Pick up that fucking No. 3, Paul.' 'You're a wee c**t, Paul.'

Despite the Shire's frailties on the flanks, they looked likely to escape with a draw. Scott Livingstone equalised, McGrillen made it 2-1, but then Ross Donaldson equalised with a fluked shot-cum-cross. Donaldson had been getting the inevitable stick about his inability to score goals and quite naturally turned to the away dugout to look for some sort of approval. But the manager had missed his moment of glory. He had been lecturing Graham McGhee about the art of full-back play and Paul Ross's deficiencies in that department. 'Who scored that?' demanded Newall. 'Ross Donaldson? About fucking time.'

Then Derek Jackson got injured. He hobbled around on one leg for a few minutes, but it was plain he could not carry on. 'Where's Cat?' barked the manager. 'Get Cat on.' The Cat, however, was nowhere to be found. We were about to assemble a search party when someone spotted him taking a leak on an advertising hoarding in a distant corner of the ground. There was an even longer delay while we waited for him to go through his psyching-up routine. 'Watch this,' said Newall, as the keeper lined up his first goalkick. 'It won't reach the edge of the area. See this one? This will come back with snow on it.'

The Cat, however, could not be blamed for McGrillen's winning goal. The Shire defence was nowhere as the tiny winger headed in from close range bang on ninety minutes. Again. When I left, a gentleman, wearing an official Stenhousemuir tie, was begging McGrillen, on his way out of the front door with a round object bulging out of his kit bag, to return the match ball.

The prospect of a 190-mile round trip into the wilds of Angus on a Tuesday night in March sparked an epidemic of illness and injury at Firs Park with the cry-offs for the Montrose game in double figures. Derek Rae could justifiably have joined them as this was the game that clashed with the imminent birth of his daughter. He travelled with the team; definitely beyond the call of his tenner a week.

Newall was away on business in Milan, and with Denham on the field in the No. 5 jersey the reserve striker, Gordon Parks, found himself suddenly elevated to the role of manager. That made me, I supposed, assistant manager, a frightening thought. What if Parks decided to put himself on as a sub? Still, if nothing else I did manage to perfect the nonchalant lean against the dugout.

Parks appeared willing to accept his limitations: 'I can't

RK HERALD

VERY THURSDAY

PLAYERS &
OFFICIALS ONLY

Top: Les Thomson sorts out the wages in his chief executive's office, hoping he has enough pound coins to give each player ten.

Right: Stairway to Heaven: Alex Forsyth and Ross 'Doughnuts' Strang at the Directors' Entrance. Behind him, a steward bars a gatecrasher. Has he come to the wrong ground?

Previous page: The Dead End Kids – acerbic, sceptical and very, very funny.

Top left: Striker Derek Ure, local lad made good, checking to see if his mum made it through the crowds in time for kick-off.

Top right: Bucket and Spade, Paul and Mark Tyrell, were two of the Shire's best signings.

Let battle commence: Stephen Oates and Scott Livingstone.

Greig Denham gets overheated. Dennis Newall stays unusually cool.

All action at the Firs Street end, with as many players as fans.

Chairman of the Board, Alan J. Mackin, captured on camera during a rare visit to Firs Park.

When push came to shove the Shire could always rely on Ross Donaldson.

Top left: Goalkeeper Derek Jackson looks for divine help on the way to a half-time bollocking, Steven Oates keeps his head down, Mark Tyrell ruminates.

Top right: Cheeky chappie Johnny Walker and Graham 'Gee' McGhee, captains past and present.

Left: Paul Ross: in the dug-out and the doghouse.

Left: The bonniest security in Britain keep a watch in the main stand.

Next page: The birds have flown. Emu and *Loaded* friend lament the home loss to Cowdenbeath. The blow-up doll takes it lying down.

Below: Bob the Builder and the Laughing Policeman lead the chorus as the *Loaded* gang get loaded at Firs Park.

get a game and I'm picking the team,' he said. Well, not quite; we had an open hotline – mobile to mobile – to Milan. Dennis had kept a grip on the reins. From 3,000 miles away, he told Paul Ross what was required of him. When Chris McGroarty put the Shire ahead after eleven minutes all sorts of alarming prospects must have opened in his mind. What, for example, if we were to win? Would he find himself out on his ear? Would Chairman Mackin appoint the new Parks and Connor management team? Would he be offering them a long-term contract, company car and a rented bolt-hole in Falkirk?

Newall needn't have worried. A violent snowstorm swept in from the Angus hills and somewhere in the white-out Montrose were scoring four goals without reply. Even changing the white ball for an orange one failed to make a difference. And the manager's absence failed to give his players a rest from his verbal assaults. Down the line from Italy came his familiar voice, the familiar imprecations, the choreographed insults, the pre-ordained bollockings: 'Tell Ross Donaldson he is a fat, lazy t**t and he has to up his work-rate.' 'Paul Ross, squeeze up.' 'Get someone to take the line-kicks for Cat. He couldn't kick a dead cow.'

It was like Groundhog Day. And it was infectious. Parks put on his best Dennis Newall face and language in the dressing room and gave Paul Ross a bollocking. Ross responded by announcing that he was quitting 'this fucking shite outfit'. One game in and the new management team had managed to lose three points and a player. I blamed Parks of course.

The final trip to Elgin brought another 8 a.m. start with players yawning their way on to the bus and immediately falling asleep. But more problems we could have all done without.

Dennis's mother was in intensive care in Livingston with respiratory problems. It did not stop him travelling, although he did take his BMW in case he had to do a swift U-turn. He trailed Mr Bryan and his bus at 50 m.p.h. all the way to Elgin, alternately swearing at the endless roadworks and checking his mobile for the dreaded call.

Ross Donaldson had decided he would meet us at Elgin. He was working up there, he told the manager, and he had to go to a shop-opening. The opening was too good to miss: 'Aye, that'll be a Burger King shop, then?' Chief executive Les Thomson was also absent – his mother-in-law had died during the week – and there was no Bobby Jack, either – he had marital problems and no-one knew where he was.

I knew what was coming next and, sure enough, Jimmy Wilson informed me with due gravitas: 'Bobby's awa', so you are now the assistant kitman. You've been promoted.' He may have seen this as promotion, but four days previously I had been doing my best impersonation of Jose Mourinho, long leather coat and all. To be honest, I saw it more as a sideways move at best. One moment management material, the next kitman (assistant).

The good news was that Paul Ross had had a change of heart and had decided to stay with his 'shite outfit'. ('He needs the status that playing for the Shire gives him,' explained Gordon Parks, without a trace of irony.) And the Shire produced one of their better displays at Elgin to force a 0-0 draw. Parks got on in the last minute and missed a sitter, which just about illustrated the fickle nature of football with the Shire; one day a chief, the next a bloody useless Indian.

At least I couldn't really go wrong in my new role as kitman (assistant), although I had to bury a few sensibilities. I felt a deep sense of moral outrage as the players flung to the floor the jerseys I had carefully laid out in immaculate order ninety minutes earlier. Ross Donaldson, undergoing his ritual verbal disembowelment at the hands of Dennis, spat into the pile; another player gargled the contents of a water bottle over it. I decided that I wasn't cut out for the job and was about to tell Jimmy Wilson exactly that when he forestalled me. 'You're no giving the job enough,' he said.

'Are you firing me?' I asked hopefully.

'You are fired,' he told me.

On the trip home the away fans, as always, found some statistical consolation for travelling so far for so little: their team had now amassed the same number of points as two years ago, in the Danny Diver era. And there were still ten matches to go.

David Bingham is the hustler of the murky pool halls of Scottish football. Fast Eddie Felson, that's who he is. A man who has been around, walked away from the big time (Dunfermline, Livingston, Inverness Caley Thistle) and now makes a killing making chumps of his inferiors – the clueless journeymen, the bit-part players of the Third Division.

Watching him pull the hapless Shire apart with the meticulous callousness of a little boy pulling the wings off a fly, one could only tip a hat towards a footballer who, at the age of thirty-three, has played the system to perfection. Bingham had been to one of my book launches in Inverness and shops, unrecognised, at my local Tesco in Edinburgh. He usually says hello and seems a nice guy. But you have to question his astonishing lack of ambition. Many people in the game do just that.

'See that David Bingham?' said Newall before the match. 'You have to question a guy who could be up in Aberdeen

playing in the SPL for Inverness Caley and yet he's at Firs
Park playing East Stirling. This is a guy who played for
Scotland. But if you put a chequebook in front of someone
they'll jump.'

Gretna were going up all right. They had clinched
promotion to Division Two the previous Saturday at
Cowdenbeath, but as with all sporting teams built on the
benevolence of a single man (Jack Walker at Blackburn,
Roman Abramovich at Chelsea, Vladimir Romanov at Heart
of Midlothian) there seemed to be a tangible feeling of
impermanence about them.

Gretna don't have much in the way of an indigenous
support and their home gate averaged around 300 despite
the fact that fans can expect, on any given Saturday, victory by a large margin. For the momentous match at
Cowdenbeath, fewer than 100 had travelled. They couldn't
muster the numbers to justify a bus for the Firs Park fixture.

Newall had delivered the perfect team talk – for the opposition – when he had gone on the record, in the *Scottish
Sun*, and insisted that Gretna's tactics of buying anything
worthwhile that moved in the lower divisions had 'devalued'
the league. The tabloids have an uncanny ability to turn a
mundane remark into a major insult, but he really should
have known better.

As it was, Gretna were two up in no time at all and even
Newall had to admit that they could play. Their forward line
featured at No. 9 the division's leading scorer, Kenny Deuchar,
who is a GP in real life; surprisingly, he is known as The
Doc. A number of identical bleach-blond fliers, swift and
athletic, feasted voraciously on Bingham's feel for space. The
visitors went on to win 4-0 and their only hiccup came when
defender Andy Aitken, the last man in defence, was red-
carded after a collision with Ross Donaldson. 'Going down,

going down, going down,' the Dead End Kids sang at the champions.

The Shire tried, but could barely lay a boot on Bingham; he was never in possession long enough. He was like one of those ringers that turn up on the opposition side at your weekly five-a-side game. You want to kick him up in the air, but can't get near him.

Good as he might have been, though, he did eventually get his come-uppance. Midway through the second half, the Shire captain Johnny Walker, tormented to distraction, brought him down with a rugby tackle. Bingham fell heavily on his hand and was led off in obvious pain. The anxious faces in the Gretna dugout said just about everything about the player's value to the team.

'Have you got a doctor?' bawled the Gretna physio at the Shire dugout, barely able to contain his panic. Yeah right. The Shire have a club doctor.

'Nah, we've nae doctor,' said Newall.

'Oh God, what am I meant to do now?'

'Why don't you get your centre-forward to look at him?' I asked. Genius, I know.

'For fuck's sake, never thought of that,' said the physio.

Newall's hate figure for the night, following the strict rota that featured Ross Donaldson and, when he was fit, Chris Baldwin, was Paul Ross. One could only wonder if the 'status' of playing for the Shire was adequate compensation. Newall's rant at all things Paul Ross lasted from the opening minute, through the half-time 'pep talk' where Donaldson and Greig Denham almost came to blows, until a minute from time when stadium announcer Les Mitchell's voice came over the tannoy to proclaim: 'And the Gordon Lounge Shire Man of the Match for tonight is . . . Paul Ross.' All of us in the dugout turned in unison to look at the manager. For once in his life, Dennis Newall was speechless.

Bingham, it was discovered later, had chipped a bone in his hand. Fast Eddie went home with the money all right, but he also got his fingers broke.

 # THE GREEN SHOOTS
OF RECOVERY

Gretna's consummate performance, their skill and sheer professionalism must have rubbed off, and for seven glorious days in March the Shire actually began to look, and perform . . . well, like a football team. This was due in no small part to the influence of the new arrivals, Chris McGroarty and the brothers, Bucket and Spade, Tyrell.

The Firs Park mud suited The Tank down to the ground. It was the time of the year for big legs and little subtlety, although it could be argued that the three back-to-back home wins were achieved in gluepot conditions which brought every visiting team down to our level. But it was apparent that the Tyrells, McGroarty and the veteran goalkeeper Derek Jackson have been inspired signings, as Dennis Newall modestly admitted.

On the face of it, McGroarty had been a real coup. He had made over 100 starts for Dunfermline in the SPL. It was rumoured that he had once been a target for Celtic, but after a change in management at Dunfermline his career had declined. He had loan spells at Clyde and St Mirren, brief visits to Airdrie and Dumbarton and had begun the dreaded, concentric progress back into the divisions. Now he was as low as you could go, at the age of twenty-four.

Originally from Bellshill, he had hair dyed white blond and pinched, anaemic features. His undoubted skills had the home fans in raptures; like many class players, he always seemed to have time on the ball, not a widespread commodity in the Scottish Third Division. He was what managers like to call a model professional and, like the Tyrells and Jackson, listened intently to everything that Dennis Newall had to say. McGroarty also worked wonders for club bean counters wherever he went, followed as he was by a large family group. It was said he had turned down a contract with Lincoln City in England's Division Three and I wondered why.

The hat-trick of home wins were heartening in every sense. There was now a real possibility that the voyage to the bottom of the league could be avoided and, as the Shire statisticians pointed out, it was the first time since 2002 that the club had managed three wins on the bounce. I wasn't so sure – my guess was that surely the previous time must have been around about the Battle of Falkirk.

But the Shire had also broken new ground and added three new names to the list of teams they had beaten. In the last three seasons they had only managed victories against Queen's Park and Elgin City. Now Stenhousemuir, Cowdenbeath and East Fife had been added to the Third Division's roll of dishonour.

For obvious reasons, this did not go down too well with these clubs. All three managers, as is the wont of managers, happily trotted out familiar excuses: an injury list, key players banned, a long, hard season and above all, the state of the Firs Park field – or rather swamp – of play.

For visiting fans, too, a beating by the Shire was hard to take. Too hard for some. During the 2-1 win over Cowdenbeath there was a sobering, Millwall moment when the under-worked Firs Park stewards had to be aroused from their slumbers to quell an outpouring of discontent on the five-yard square of terracing containing the visiting fans.

When things kick off in the crowd at Firs Park, they really kick off. The linesman on the far side had been pelted with nothing less than spent chewing gum and the security had to move in *en masse* and with haste. Packets of Wrigleys spearmint were confiscated and, against the odds, the match, and the linesman, carried on untroubled.

Dennis Newall had another reason for beating Cowdenbeath, apart from the fact that they were sitting third in the league, had won their last three games, and, according to him at any rate, 'were getting too big for their fucking boots'. His son Chris had fallen out with the manager, Dave Baikie, and had been released. Like dad, he was desperate to see his former club humiliated. Dennis was trying hard to get his son back to Firs Park, without success. So it was a double-whammy for the Newall family when the Shire produced one of their best performances of the season.

Cowdenbeath did take an early lead when Derek Jackson failed to cut out a difficult cross and the ball dropped obligingly at the feet of the nearest striker, who tapped it in. 'See if that had been us,' lamented Newall with some justification, 'the ball would have hit a defender and bounced clear.'

The manager's eternal scapegoat, Paul Ross, got some of his Brownie points back a few minutes later by clearing off his own line. He knocked himself out on the upright in the process and this evidence of commitment not only earned the little midfielder some rare praise from the manager at half-time but also seemed to rouse something within his side.

Three minutes into the second half, striker Derek Ure caused havoc in the visiting defence with a storming run and McGroarty found time and space to beat two defenders before scoring. The winner arrived on the hour mark when a poor clearance from the Cowdenbeath defence at a corner was turned into the box by Scott Livingstone and The Tank's header gave the Shire only their third win bonus of the season.

Against Stenhousemuir the new model Shire – running, fighting, ploughing through the Firs Park mud and, above all, finally believing in themselves – surpassed even that performance.

Ross Donaldson, in his element in the quagmire where he was no longer the slowest man on the park, spun daintily to side-foot into the net. McGroarty got a second. Stenhousemuir got back into the game with a freaky lob that Jackson, looking strangely fallible, seemed to have covered – but it slid into the net off his gloves. The Shire's third was a long shot from Paul Ross that took a deflection that totally deceived the keeper. For once in their lives, the Shire appeared to be getting the rub of the green and could even afford to miss a penalty when Ure was upended in the box; McGroarty's spot-kick was saved.

The visitors scored a second after a prolonged scramble in the home penalty area, but with Hamlet smoke puffing out of Dennis Newall's ears with the gusto of a Grangemouth chimney, the clock ran down. The Shire were safe.

The win over the 'local' rivals provoked another outbreak of generosity from the main sponsors. Littlewoods, to celebrate 'our third win of the season' promised half-price entry for the East Fife match on 19 March. All the fans had to do was produce a voucher which could be found in the latest edition of the *Falkirk Herald*. Considering the unexpected win bonuses that the Shire were clocking up, this was generosity indeed and the local convenience stores were swamped by fans eager to take advantage of this £4 saving.

At Tesco, in the central retail park, the newspaper kiosk

was almost overrun. *Herald* sales were going through the roof, but there was no sign of the voucher. Someone had forgotten to inform the newspaper. As the referee raised his whistle to his lips to signal the start of the game, a queue of around thirty frustrated fans – a multitude by the normal standards of Firs Park – congregated at the turnstiles, all unwilling to pay the full £8.

There were muttered threats, the turnstile operators were in danger of being lynched, the stewards called club offic-ials, the club officials called Littlewoods. The gatemen stood firm: 'You can only come in for £4 if you have the voucher frae the *Herald*,' the angry mob was told.

Finally, as the howls of frustration grew louder and louder, it was decided to let the fans in for £4. Inevitably, all the fans inside who had paid the full amount then laid siege to the harassed turnstile attendants – and demanded £4 back. At half-time Les Mitchell, possibly on the orders of the club, went on the tannoy to tell the unhappy masses that 'it's not the fault of Littlewoods and it's not the fault of the turn-stile operators or the club, it's the fault of someone at the *Falkirk Herald*'. Very noble, I thought.

East Fife had also been tapping into a rich vein of form but they, too, met their match at Firs Park where, not for the first time, conditions underfoot put skill at a premium and nullified the visitors' long ball game. It does help if the ball bounces on landing.

The visitors began with a flourish but the Shire took con-trol. Paul Ross, rapidly becoming Newall's blue-eyed boy – to the surprise of both – began the move that led to the only goal when he released Scott Livingstone on the right side of the penalty area. His cross was met by Derek Ure, who fired a low hard drive past the East Fife goalkeeper.

The haplessness that once affected the Shire was now

apparently affecting the opposition. Their centre-forward headed wide of the goal from three yards and, in the closing minutes, Jackson pulled off a fine save to deny them again.

Everything was unexpectedly sunny in the Shire garden. As the team and fans celebrated the three-in-a-row, the Scottish newspapers carried a report from the Football League's eight-man management committee. They were to put forward a proposal to the general meeting in May, which basically secured a future for the Shire in Division Three. They would be given, effectively, another four years' grace to get off the bottom. Second bottom would be good enough.

Under the rule, any club who finished last two years in a row – the Shire in other words – would be reduced from full to associate members, and surrender their voting rights. They would then be given a two-year probationary period to convince everyone they deserved to be retained.

As the legislation would not be retrospective, the Shire would remain an entry on the fixture lists until the summer of 2009 at the very least. All that was required was a two-thirds majority of member clubs. They were saved, all they needed now was somewhere to play.

As if on cue, a new message appeared in the 'latest news' section of the Shire website. 'Firs Park statement,' it read. 'The board of directors wish to announce that the club will continue to play its football at Firs Park until at least the end of the 2005/6 season, as the conditional contract for the sale of Firs Park has not yet been confirmed. The board is still committed to finding a solution to the issue of a permanent and financially viable home for the club. A further announcement will be made in due course.' Mackin's ground sale, at least for the time being, had fallen through.

10

PARTY POOPERS

One step forward, three steps back. The unprecedented four-in-a-row was stymied on 2 April at Queen's Park, who managed to avoid the unwanted fate of being tagged as 'The Shire fall guys after Elgin' by winning 2-0.

We had been granted the previous Saturday off because Scotland were playing a World Cup qualifier against Italy in the San Siro Stadium on 26 March, the hope presumably being that the population of Falkirk would decamp *en masse* to Milan. Scotland had been 14/1 against to win – about the same odds as you could get for the Shire winning four times in succession. But they had already won three on the bounce and Queen's Park had failed to score in four matches. The bookies were quivering.

But the break seemed to have done the Shire more harm than good, because after twenty minutes of concerted pressure the home side managed their first goal in over 400 minutes of football. Another followed at the start of the second half. The victory roll was over, but not the desperate, and often bitter, battle with Albion Rovers to avoid the Third Division wooden spoon. A win the following weekend at Montrose was now a must.

On the bus up to Angus there was one notable absentee; Gordon Parks, part-time footballer and full-time *Daily Record* reporter, had been given the elbow. Again. But this time it wasn't a suspension, it was permanent.

Apparently, after the previous dispute, Mackin had been promised £2,000 by the newspaper for the honour of having the Shire's deeds documented in Parks's Monday column. The *Record* had reneged once again. Parks, who like every other player at the Shire, simply cannot live without football (he had been a noted striker in Divisions One and Two), wrote a personal cheque for £2,000, from an out-of-date chequebook, as a guarantee. He asked Les Thomson not to cash it. Thomson paid it straight into the bank and the cheque bounced. So did Parks. Jim Traynor, Park's boss at the *Record*, had to offer a grovelling apology – and agreed to pay the club something.

Amazingly, he was told that the deal had been for £10,000 – plus a tractor mower for Jimmy Wilson. I thought of my first meeting with Mackin and felt a moment of empathy with Scotland's indigenous red-top. In the end, Traynor and the Shire settled for £1,000.

Links Park, Montrose, has arguably the best Third Division facilities outside Hampden Park, and unarguably the best pies served by the most cheerful serving ladies. The fans are friendly, too. One was happy to show me round and inform me that a normal home gate would attract around 500. Pre-season friendlies against Aberdeen and Dundee United, and derby games against Arbroath – the obligatory bitter local rivals, although Arbroath always claim that fixtures against Brechin City are more meaningful – always attracted four-figure crowds.

The club, known as the Gable Endies, had just celebrated their 125th anniversary and the friendly fan's summary of that century-and-a-quarter could serve as a microcosm of Scottish football: 'We are survivors. We have had money and spent it. We have been broke and we have had success and we have had failure, more failure than success I would say. But, we are still here and that's all that counts. And Montrose is a bonny wee place.'

I had time on my hands before the kick-off. 'Anything worth seeing in Montrose?'

'Well, there's the harbour. That's bonny, And there's the parish church, that's a famous local landmark. That's bonny too. The steeple is over 200 feet tall. Look, you can actually see it from here.'

'And what do they say round here about the church and its steeple?' I invited.

'They don't say anything about it,' he replied, puzzled.

I walked into town with Jimmy Wilson, bought him a pie at a High Street chippie and he brought me up to date on his groundsman travails.

Bobby was back, but Daft Dougie was away and in his place Jimmy had had a new 'deputy assistant groundsman', supplied by the employment agency of Polmont Young Offenders' Institute. Malcy was another small Glasgow ned with a chilling smile and he had told Jimmy on his first day that he was the nephew of the notorious Glasgow gangster T. C. Campbell, fresh out of the nick for his supposed part in the city's Ice Cream Wars. He was also related to the minder of Paul Ferris, another noted No Mean City hard man.

Campbell had just been released after serving a seventeen-year prison term. Six members of the Doyle family had perished in their tenement flat in Ruchazie, targeted, it was alleged, because they refused to give up their ice cream van route in Garthamlock. Many ice cream vans were believed to be used as a front for selling drugs. Campbell had been wrongly convicted, but his name still had, shall we say, a certain resonance. I couldn't wait to tell Dennis Newall the news. 'Does that mean we'll get 99s at half-time now?' he asked. Then: 'What's the lad doing time for anyway?'

'Attempted murder, apparently.'

The manager thought for a moment. 'Has he ever played football?'

A Derek Ure header gave Shire an unexpected lead before the inevitable reply on the stroke of half-time (the Shire and the referee's glance at his watch have a fatal ambience). After that it was one-way traffic with the veteran Shire keeper Derek Jackson having a horribly flawed game.

At half-time Ross Donaldson, by way of his input into the dressing-room discussions, informed us that a Montrose player had called us 'a pub team' and that 'he would shove it down their throats'. In the second half Donaldson was then sent off for, well, a pub team foul and Montrose poured forwards on the Shire goal. The second came nine minutes into the half, the third on sixty-two minutes, and six minutes from the end Jackson sclaffed a goal-kick straight to a Montrose player and he gobbled up the unexpected gift.

Jackson was gutted and, after the usual Dennis diatribe, cleared his throat and spoke up: 'I am forty in August. I have a good job and could call it a day. But I love this game. I came here from Sauchie Juniors and they paid me well, but it is not senior football. This means everything to me and I hold up my hands and apologise to everyone, my fellow players, the manager and the fans. The Shire support gave me some stick and I deserve it. It will take me until Monday to get this out of my system. I will get some stick at work but I will put this all behind me. I will be back in training, I will play next week and I will do better. All of us have to look at ourselves and decide what we want out of this, out of the rest of the season.'

There didn't seem much more to say after that, although

most of the Shire players were astonished to discover that their last line of defence was nearly forty. And Ross Donaldson caused a major diplomatic incident by asking if they would be able to stop for a carry-out on the way home. 'A fucking carry-out?' bawled the manager. 'You get a carry-out when you win something. See you, Ross, you got sent off and now you think you can celebrate! That's our first red card of the season. You should be hanging your head in shame.'

On the way home to Edinburgh late that night I passed Westfield Stadium. The hated Falkirk had won at home, again, and earned promotion. The car park was still full. A white stretch limo was parked outside the players' entrance. Yogi Hughes had his lift home. And Falkirk, or rather Grangemouth, had an SPL team.

The Montrose defeat had a number of remarkable after-effects. On a link on their supporters' website, Gable Graffiti, the following message appeared which I reproduce in all its glory:'Regina versus Ross Donaldson, before Lord Chief Justice Steeplejack. Rutherglen man Ross Donaldson (23) was arraigned yesterday on charges of fraudulently impersonating a footballer. A stream of witnesses for the crown denounced Donaldson variously as "a hod carrier" and "the poor man's Grant Mitchell". The prosecution alleged that, on Saturday last, Donaldson intimidated employees of East Stirlingshire FC into allowing him to take the pitch wearing their No. 9 shirt, and further, that he extorted from them a contract paying £10 per week. Donaldson's fraud was unmasked as soon as he took the pitch and quickly began sweating out Friday night's 19 pints of Stella. The judge ordered Donaldson tagged and banned him from a ten-mile radius surrounding Firs Park. The shamefaced Donaldson was further ordered to pay back the sum of £61.90 plus VAT, which represented his season's wages extorted to date.'

Monday night training was dominated by meetings. The players held their own in a locked dressing room to do what Jackson had suggested and 'look within themselves'. The management team convened in Newall's office to decide who was going and who was staying at the end of the season, and the Shire Supporters' Club had their own get-together in the Sticky Carpet to which Dennis Newall, Greig Denham and myself had been invited.

It had been almost a full season since the last management/fans' meet, and the Shire had actually won a few games since. The mood was upbeat among the usual suspects, this time with four extra bodies present. Dennis and Greig answered everything with grace and humour, the manager made them smile with a couple of jokes and even the disgruntled regular (denied his bar space earlier by the Shire fans' early season meeting) again looking to reclaim his favoured seat failed to spoil the accord. It was agreed by all that Newall and Denham had 'worked a miracle'.

'Do you think we can get off the bottom now?' one fan asked of Dennis. To which he responded encouragingly: 'Well, it's Albion Rovers this weekend, the boys have got Montrose out of their systems and there has been a positive mood all week. I tell you what, if we don't it won't be for want of trying.' This was it. The moment when boys could become men and men could walk tall in the knowledge they had responded to the challenge before them. Success in the shape of a second bottom finish was a real possibility. If they could overcome Albion. Defeat would destroy the dream for another season.

Talk, however, is clearly cheap, as the match against second-bottom Rovers proved. All the promises to look within themselves, all the vows to try harder, came to nothing in a dreadful match enlivened only be the ferocity of some of the challenges. Ross Donaldson had copped a three-match ban – Gable Graffiti had that bit right – Shaggy was in Norway for his father's sixty-fifth birthday celebrations and the bench was threadbare. Even the physio was missing. And, after the team's glorious March, the gods of football had turned against the Shire again.

At Montrose, Jimmy Wilson had told me a story about Daft Dougie. I don't know if it is true or not but, apparently, one weekend his girlfriend had announced, out of the blue, that she 'wanted a bit of a change'. She fancied a three-some. 'The Daft one couldnae concentrate on his job after that,' said Jimmy.

A terrible thought struck me. What if Jimmy had asked the deputy assistant groundsman to get rid of a few offending divots on the playing surface and what if Daft Dougie's mind was elsewhere and he missed one? And what if the Shire goalkeeper attempted a clearance, only for the ball to bobble on the offending divot and straight to an opposing player?

Sure enough, a few minutes into the Rovers game when Derek Jackson's attempted clearance took a horrible bounce, the ball landed obligingly at the feet of the opposition centre-forward, who scored. The Shire, who had suffered all manner of perversities in their 124-year history had seemingly broken new ground and become the first football club ever to lose a game on account of a *ménage à trois*. I could see the headline in the *Scottish Sun*: 'OH FORK! THREE IN A BED ROMP COSTS SHIRE DEAR'.

The second Rovers goal was a simple one-two which 'an Under-11 defence could have read', according to Greig Denham. The Shire were beaten, could not, even by a mathematical miracle avoid last place for the third successive season, and were once again officially Britain's Worst Football Team™.

At the end, apart from his time-honoured rant at Paul Ross ('I'm in the mood to put you through that wall, you little c**t'), Dennis Newall was almost resigned. 'You've fucked up again. We are bottom again. There's not a lot more I can do,' he informed his charges. They hung their heads and tried to look shamefaced, but I could sense their relief that the season was almost over.

When the sopping wet jerseys, muddied shorts and discarded tie-ups had been swept away and the players had melted into the night I noticed some new graffiti on a fixture list pinned to the wall. 'THE GAFFER'S A PRICK' some anonymous, and presumably departed, player had scrawled in pencil in capital letters. I thought of telling Dennis, but maybe the time wasn't right.

The Shire's fourth local derby of the season was marked by a home display of mind-numbing ineptitude made notable only by the performance of Mark, the Firs Park gateman. This was his moment of glory. With Stenhousemuir leading 4-1 and the Shire fans already drifting away to the Sticky Carpet, their goalkeeper gathered the ball on the edge of his area, stepped over the white line defining his territory and was immediately sent off by an unforgiving referee.

The offender was reluctant to depart and suddenly, for only the second time that season, we had what the sporting hacks would describe as 'a flashpoint'. Mark the gateman's reaction was instantaneous. Wobbling away from his usual station by the Shire pie wagon, he called in the troops. Big Mal was dispatched to the far side of the ground to forestall the anticipated pitch invasion by the eight travelling Stenhousemuir fans (or seven if you discount the seven-month-old baby wheeled on to the ground in a pram by his father). The other stewards were ordered to 'stand by' and Mark positioned himself by the players' entrance in case the

Stenhousemuir keeper attempted to demolish the stand – or maybe the referee – on his way off.

Nearby, a Japanese tourist, who had run out of things to do and see in Falkirk and somehow found his way into Firs Park, looked on in bemusement.

With such iron-clad precautions in place, the situation quickly defused itself. To everyone's relief. Except, perhaps, the Dead End Kids'.

The match itself had a distinct end-of-term feel about it. In the Shire dressing room, someone had made away with one of Dennis's round discs from the magnetic playboard and the manager raised a laugh by saying: 'Well, Ross Donaldson is suspended, after all.'

Outside, there was some jocular badinage between both dugouts and even a friendly linesman joined in. David Jenkins, the physio, informed me that he was going to invoke the copyright act over Derek Jackson, the goalkeeper. Both liked to be called DJ, but 'I wus here first,' says DJ Mark 1.

The smiles in the home dugout swiftly faded, though, as the Shire somehow surpassed themselves in their sheer awfulness. DJ, the goalkeeper, set the tone early on when he got down to gather an innocuous long-range shot only to see the ball take an obscene bounce off a rogue divot (Daft Dougie strikes again) and fly over his head and into the net. It was all downhill, again, from there.

Chris McGroarty, the Shire's one player of true class, had a stinker and although nineteen-year-old Grant Findlay earned a start in front of his proud dad in place of the suspended Donaldson, his only reward was a booking, a clash of heads that left him with a bruise the size of a golf ball on the side of his head . . . and a bollocking from the manager.

Paul Ross, Dennis's traditional dumping ground for opprobrium, was singled out yet again . . . although he hadn't even played. Apparently, he had 'showed fuck-all enthusiasm in the pre-match warm-up'. Ross, who on recent Saturdays had showed a heartening willingness to stand up to the Gaffer and argue the toss, didn't even bother to reply. He was speechless.

In the background, the flushing toilets and spin drier competed with Dennis's rantings, but one message did come over loud and clear: 'There are too many in here happy to take the second prizes.' For Greig Denham, his assistant, the Shire had 'too many losers'.

On the way down the corridor I passed Adele, John Morton's daughter, who was emerging from the manager's office. I went in to find a single meat pie on Dennis Newall's desk. His post-match banquet.

'Sha la la la la la la la! Sha la la la la la la la!' There were roadworks on the M74, Ross Donaldson was missing again and we had to make the tour of Falkirk to pick up the chief executive outside his home. Tony Christie was once again on Radio One showing us the way to Amarillo. Or rather the way to Gretna. Sweet FA waited for us there. The sense of *déjà vu* was almost overpowering.

But Mr Bryan's bus had new faces on board this time. It was like a jolly works' outing. Aside from the usual duo of Alex Forsyth and John Morton, Morton's daughter, Adele, and two extra passengers were making the trip. Colin, a friend of DJ's (the physio one) from Glen Ochil prison, was riding with us, along with the Mark the gateman, this presumably being the reward for his season's labours. Although still dressed in his bouncer's colours – black – he was in a sunny mood and even spoke a few words to me. I couldn't make out what he said, but it certainly wasn't 'Got a ticket, mate?'

Colin, who made up a small clique of turnkeys along

with DJ the Goalie, slept all the way there and all the way back. For all I know he may have slept through the match.

DJ the Goalie had been in the news during the week, giving an unguarded interview to the *Scottish Sun* in which he revealed that he had two gay dogs as pets. It also transpired that he was once man of the match for Arbroath in a 13-1 Scottish Cup defeat by Celtic. DJ the Physio, who liked to remind him of his veteran status by helpfully filling in his Saga holiday forms for him, told me that in the manner of so many goalkeeping eccentrics, DJ the Goalie began his career as an attacking midfielder.

At Strathclyde Country Park we picked up the Glasgow contingent and the management team. Dennis Newall had some startling news: not only had he binned Ross Donaldson, permanently, for missing training, but Greig Denham had decided to leave the club at the end of the season.

Greig, who didn't seem too overwrought by his decision, told me the club had refused to pay the £590 for his SFA coaching B certificate, as demanded by the Scottish Football League. On the face of it, this seemed an appalling way to treat a man who had given so much time to a lost cause, but as Thomson had just opened a letter containing a bill for £550 from Scottish Water it was hardly surprising. Mackin had made the decision from his villa in Majorca, leaving Les Thomson to tell Greig in person.

Greig already had another club lined up. Dennis had another assistant waiting in the wings and for the first time the manager wrote down the team line on his piece of paper without consulting his assistant. They sat apart.

As for the Shire's burly cult hero, Donaldson had wanted a week off to go to his caravan, Dennis had refused and the striker had responded by cutting training. Now he was out the door. I suspected Dennis would miss him, we all would, but as he pointed out: 'Three goals in a season from a guy who is supposed to be a striker is fuck all.'

On the way down we all voted for the players' player of the year on torn-up pieces of A4 paper. Dennis Newall's, I noted, read: 'No Fucker.'

Despite the roadworks we arrived early and decided to kill time in a pub by the ground. The startled landlord, busy pouring an eighty-year-old regular a large Scotch, was confronted by his dream scenario – twenty-two newcomers all looking for soft drinks.

On the side of the bar someone had hung an ancient bell, presumably used to signal time. I pointed out the inscription on it to Les Thomson, who was busy picking up the tab. 'Titanic 1912', it said. Les didn't seem to appreciate the implied irony. He didn't laugh. Nor did he laugh when two large men with red boozers' faces, seated in the beer garden outside, asked where we were from.

'East Stirlingshire,' said Thomson quietly.

'Where?'

'East Stirlingshire.'

'Oh that load of shite,' said one.

Last time, on the Day of Diversion, it had been 8-1 and in the intervening eight months Gretna had won the Third Division championship in a canter, amassing ninety-eight points from thirty-six games. The last half-dozen games had given them a return of six wins, with a goals for tally of twenty-seven, goals against three. The Shire were to be the tasty little entrée at Brooks Mileson's championship banquet.

The programme notes from Rowan Alexander announced the extent of his achievements. Along with the usual dire warning about the perils of not taking the Shire seriously, the Gretna manager listed: Goals for (so far) 124, goals against 29. Games won (so far) 30. Drawn 2, lost 2. Thirty-four full-time professionals, ten youth professionals. Top goalscorer in Scotland, Kenny Deuchar; Third Division Player of the Year, David Bingham. Bryan Gilfillan was a Northern Ireland Under-21 international and the club had the highest crowd average in the Third Division for 2004/5 (albeit 300). Then, intriguingly and possibly as some sort of private joke, Alexander had added: 'Most prolific goalscorer in the world, K. Deuchar.' The Gretna manager concluded by asking: 'And people still knock us?'

Well, they certainly did that. They had been called everything from a team of mercenaries to Big Time Billys. Most of their envious Division Three rivals had spent the season moaning about how easy it would be to manage a team that contained Bingham, Townsley, Baldocchino, et al. Naturally, at Raydale Park they saw things differently.

One regular there – and throughout the season, as I've said before, it was always a simple matter to find an obliging regular willing to spout homilies about their home-town team – told me that Mileson was 'a canny man of vision'. Keen to elaborate, he continued: 'That's why people don't like us. If you're a small club, with a local fan base, you market your fan base. All the players and coaching staff go out into the local community. Brooks Mileson will have this club in the SPL within two years.' I looked round Raydale Park and the 1,500 people there to celebrate, but held my peace. Then: 'I suppose you have a similar set-up at East Stirling?' I had to admit that, no, we did not have a similar set-up at East Stirling.

The Shire may not have spoiled the Gretna championship party but they certainly threw some cold water on it. Mileson arrived like some minor royal on walkabout, chapping hands with fans on his regal process from his Aston Martin DB9 in the car park to his seat in the directors' box. Dressed in ponytail, white T-shirt under leather jacket and baggy jeans, he looked like the oldest hippy in town.

Mileson had splashed out another £3,500 from his personal fortune on a fireworks display. A gargantuan woman with rolls of fat hanging off her stomach like meat in a butcher's shop marshalled some twelve-year-old cheerleaders.

A strange amalgam of piped band and steel drums made noisy progress round the perimeter and a grinning idiot dressed as Puck, seated behind a bar on wheels, went about squirting the fans through an optic. 'Oops, missed ya,' he shrilled at Dennis Newall. The Shire manager was not amused.

Mileson had thrown open the gates and waived admittance. Peter Donald, the Scottish Football League secretary, arrived with the Third Division trophy. But the overwhelming feeling at the end was one of anticlimax. The visiting team had much to do with this.

Newall, always with a beady eye on some new form of one-upmanship, claimed he had been psyching out Rowan Alexander all week. At the SPFA dinner the previous weekend he had offered the Gretna manager a brown envelope, presumably as a bribe. It was empty.

In the away dressing room he told the Shire players he wanted them to line up and clap Gretna on to the field, Alexander and all. It was a ploy that was immediately picked up by the Shire's most famous former manager when Manchester United faced Chelsea at Old Trafford on 9 May. Gretna ran on looking determinedly nonchalant about the whole thing. Alexander, who arrived at the ground with a white carnation in his buttonhole, wagged a disapproving finger at Dennis.

The Gretna tunnel was policed by our own Mark the gateman, who seemed to have developed a conditioned reflex about his minder duties. As soon as he saw a football crowd and a bunch of players he was away. As I came up the tunnel and out on to the pitch, I thought for one dreadful moment he was going to ask for accreditation. A small boy who attempted to gain entry was ordered to 'get oot the road, son'.

Gretna were soon into their routine, feeding off Bingham and running into space. Baldocchino scored early on but the expected avalanche never came. The Shire may have never looked like scoring, but everyone, for the only time in the season, worked their collective socks off. Deuchar the Doc was frustrated into a booking – Greig Denham claimed responsibility for this for his continual haranguing of the nearside linesman – and DJ, back on top form, did the rest with a string of marvellous saves.

The sight of Townsley in the home defence seemed to bring the worst out of Greig Denham and he barracked his former team-mate incessantly. Townsley smiled his goofy smile and I was reminded of the famous Townsley story, going back to his days at Motherwell that had done the rounds of Scottish football for years. A team-mate had told him the story of the Bodies in the Loch affair. William Beggs murdered an eighteen-year-old student and dismembered his victim's body. The limbs and torso were found at Loch Lomond and the head sixty miles away in the sea off the Ayrshire coast. 'Oh, did he top himself then?' asked Townsley.

As the Gretna party got into full swing, with the players gulping champagne and photographers fighting among themselves for the best shot of Rowan Alexander and his carnation, I made my way slowly back to Mr Bryan's bus. Just past the bar, a large man with a diamond stud in one ear and a savage haircut stood in my way. He looked like Mr Incredible.

'Are you with the Shire?' he asked.

'Well, sort of.' Cautious.

'Well, you should be proud of them. That was the best defensive display we have seen here all season.'

'Well, thank you very much. I will be happy to tell the boys that.' Relieved.

'Well, you certainly made it very hard work for us. What do you do at the club, by the way?'

I thought for a moment. What exactly did I do at the club? For one wild moment I thought of claiming responsibility for the defence, but thought better of it. At every game Dennis Newall had to list the composition of the dugout at the bottom of the team sheet. Without fail, he always wrote 'J. Conner [*sic*] observer', so that was my answer, my embroidered answer. 'Well, I'm what you might call the observation coordinator.'

'Come on ta fuck! An observation coordinator? We've got everything at Gretna, but we haven't got one of them!'

Despite the defeat, it was a happy bus that headed back up the M74. Spring was in the air, we were coming out of a long, dark tunnel, one more match and it would all be over. Even Mr Bryan looked happy, and I hadn't seen him crack a smile all season.

The reason for the jollity in the back of the bus, however, soon became all too clear. Before the Gretna match one player had advised me to get some money on Queen's Park to beat Elgin City 1-0 the same day. I wondered idly why Queen's Park? Both teams had nothing left to play for and we were two games away from the close season. 'Get money on them,' said the player.

Queen's duly won 1-0 at Hampden, after having a man sent off. Football gossip spreads faster than e-mail. A couple of weeks later, the *Sunday Mail* splashed with a story about an alleged betting coup – involving Queen's Park and Elgin City. The bookies, reported the newspaper, had been taken to the cleaners. Their tenner a week apart, it was heartwarming to think that some Shire players got something out of the season.

AT THE
END OF THE DAY

At a quarter past five on the evening of 7 May I walked out into the Firs Park centre circle for the last time. The Shire's 2004/5 season had been over for thirty minutes and had ended pretty much as it had begun. In disarray. A massacre by the Blue Toon, dressing room recriminations, bowed heads and a vow from the manager that some of those heads would roll.

Just above the Land of Leather wall, the top of the away team bus was just visible as it made its way out of Falkirk and back to the north-east. Ample opportunity to reflect on their 5-1 victory and to contemplate a new life in the Bell's Scottish League Division Two. They had left the Shire far behind in every sense of the word. As had Gretna.

Maybe it was appropriate that the preppy new kids had escaped. They had paid their visit to the old folks' home, indulged the inmates briefly, and moved on. The pensioners remained, sustained only by a golden-brown imagination of times gone by. Arbroath and Berwick, two more clubs with a history more meaningful than their present and their future, would enter the sanatorium for the 2005/6 season, their respective managements perhaps already adding up the twelve points available from their four games against the Shire.

The Peterhead support had spent much of the previous ninety minutes in a state midway between rapture at the efforts and dominance of their own side and bafflement that any opposition could be so enfeebled and so self-destructive. 'You know, I almost feel sorry for them,' a middle-aged man had told his mate in the pie wagon queue at half-time.

Johnny Walker, the Shire captain, had been sent off twenty minutes into the game for persistent abuse of the officials. Poor Cat had been responsible for three of the Peterhead goals and had suffered the proverbial nightmare. When Newall, during his pre-match address, begged his defence 'to help Cat out with some of the by-kicks as we know he can't kick the ball very far', I caught the two former SPL players, Chris McGroarty and Greig Denham, exchanging knowing smiles.

The Peterhead manager had even put himself on as a second-half substitute. The Shire being prone to bad bounces of the ball in every sense, I made a small wager with myself that he would score, and he did.

'Paul Ross, are you fucking listening?' Dennis Newall began his final speech of the 2004/5 season in time-honoured fashion, but with weary resignation and far less dynamism than his first. 'Did you think you were at fucking Wembley out there?' Ross, who had made a brief appearance as a second-half substitute, said nothing.

'See under normal circumstances? I don't expect any more than that. It's the self-destruct button all the time. Tony, what about that fucking goal you palmed into the net? Eh? For fuck's sake. See effort and commitment? Decent enough. Oatesy, see the first half when we told you to go up and help Scotty? See the second half, did you do that? It's a learning curve we are all on. See the simple things? That's the difference between success and failure and out there today was a failure. Greig?'

Denham sprinkled his own farewell with a few home

truths: 'We can't expect to win games with cringeable goals like that. The second goal the boy runs off one of our players and boom! We look like a pub team half the time. Other times we play decent enough and don't look like a bottom of the league team but then, bang! someone switches off and goal. Shortly after that, another and we are fucked. It's the concentration levels all the time. At Gretna the concentration was great, everyone was doing their job, but then that bag of shite today. But I want to thank you for all your efforts. Superb. All the best for next season.'

The manager wound things up: 'The game's gone, the season's gone. We are in a healthier state than last year but finishing off like that is not good enough. That's up to me to try and get some quality in here. The ones I haven't spoken to come to the park on Monday night and I will see you one by one in the office. Get in here between half six and half seven. The rest of youse, I will send you notification about the start of pre-season. Any problems with that let me know. I expect you to be fit by August so we can get a good start and not be bottom from the start of the season. Now go away and enjoy yourselves tonight.' Then, as an afterthought – and maybe his timing could have been better here – he reminded his playing staff that training would start on 2 July. Fifty-six days of freedom before the whole painful process began again. Torremolinos and bottled San Miguel beckoned.

Outside, the old ground was bathed in sunlight, the turf almost undamaged by the ninety minutes of hectic scuffling that constitutes a Shire fixture and a seagull ruminated serenely on top of the empty, and silent, stand.

One of the Dead End Kids, who had spent much of the previous two hours chortling at the antics in front of him, was examining the autographs of every Shire player in front of the Portakabin boardroom. He had approached me at half-time, uncharacteristically coy, and asked me to collect them for him. Everyone had signed, including the manager. 'You can sell those for thousands now,' I told him. 'Aye, right,' he laughed, back in cheeky chappie mode.

At the other end of the ground, just by the condemned terraces littered by the remains of half-eaten pies, plastic cups and discarded Shire lottery tickets, Jimmy Wilson was making his measured way across his pitch after locking the Firs Street turnstiles for the last time. He had had a busy day: the pitch, the rituals with the players' kit, putting out the corner flags. Midway through the first half, fag in mouth, he had climbed into one of the Firs Street gardens in an effort to recover an over-enthusiastic clearance. Amazingly, he had got the ball back.

Now he was off to clean the boots and put the jerseys in the wash. Bobby, his assistant, was policing the dressing room, trying to ensure that the playing staff didn't elope with shirts or shorts. Some of them, as the manager had warned, would not be coming back.

I met Jimmy by the eighteen-yard line and, searching for something to say, asked him if he had been given his budget for ground improvements next season. He smiled thoughtfully. Around £200, he guessed. I shook his hand and said an awkward goodbye, feeling suddenly, and oddly, bereaved.

'What are you going to do next season,' Greig Denham had asked in the dressing room. What indeed? For ten months this dotty, hapless institution had been part of my life. In the eleven months since I had first found the entrance to the promised land and tottered down the aluminium steps of the players/directors' entrance I had seen them play three pre-season friendlies, five Cup ties and thirty-six league games, and travelled some 5,000 miles to parts of Scotland I hadn't known existed.

I had seen some players come, some players go and watched those players humiliated by the likes of the Mighty Warriors, the Gable Enders and the Spidermen at places called Ochilview, Links Park and New Bayview. The sheer impoverishment of some of the arenas visited remains difficult to describe; the appearance and demeanour of some of the fans encountered still haunt my dreams.

I had heard a thousand f-words and almost as many c-words, whether in the dressing room, on the field or in the stands. I had eaten, at a reasonable estimate, 50 meat pies, 12 sausage rolls, 20 Mars bars and downed 41 cups of Bovril. I began the season at 196lb and finished it at 202. And still I was going to miss them.

I liked the players without exception and came to admire their resilience and fortitude in the face of what were invariably appalling odds. I had come to recognise that in many ways they were corks bobbing on the tide of fortune, a collective microcosm of life. Crazy examples of the bad breaks we are all handed. I think they came to accept me, too. Some of them showed a heart-warming delight when I broke a self-imposed ordinance and actually waited outside the dressing room door to shake their hand one by one after a rare victory.

But I felt I had really arrived the day The Cat, who had not spoken two words to me all season, turned to me in the dugout and said: 'Hey, big man, look after my gloves while I go for a leak, would ya?' Now that might not sound like the grounds for a life-long friendship, but as any goalkeeper will tell you, asking someone to look after your gloves is like asking someone to hold your baby. John Burridge, the famously eccentric former Workington, Blackpool, Aston Villa, Southend, Crystal Palace, QPR, Wolves, Derby County, Sheffield United and Hibernian keeper, used to go to bed in his. I was touched beyond words. I watched The Cat's gloves like a hawk.

Like the majority of the other sceptics and provocateurs – the *Sun*, *Sunday Sport*, *Daily Record*, *Front* and *Loaded* – I had arrived at Firs Park with a self-imposed remit to scoff and deride and had bathed myself in an air of heightened contempt. But all that had changed. I had become a fan. Not a supporter in the sense that I would offer up a large part of my life to them, as so many of the Shire followers did – I could never bear the weight of expectation or the mortification – but an admirer. As players who have moved on always say of the club they left behind: 'I will always look at their results first.'

But, at the end of the day, not much else had changed. By the Shire's standards the season had been reasonably successful. They had won 5 league games, lost 24 and drawn 7, conceding 88 goals and scoring 32. The final points tally of 22 represented an almost threefold improvement on the previous season and Raith Rovers, the team supported by the Chancellor of the Exchequer, had actually finished with a worse points record. But they operated at a level two divisions higher.

In Scotland's various Cup competitions the Shire had, in the vernacular, fallen at the first hurdle and they had remained rooted to the bottom of the British senior football pile. They are still floundering in the Waters of Lethe, and seem likely to remain there for the foreseeable future. Although, as one fan pointed out shortly after the end of the season when Albion Rovers released all their players and decided to go part-time, *à la* Shire: 'Maybe we've now got a chance of getting above them next season.' There are Everests in the minds of all men.

By early May, Dennis Newall had still not been invited

to stay on for the next season. The chairman was in Scotland all right, on a flying visit, but had opted to remain in Edinburgh and watch his son win the Scottish Open tennis championships. Some would say he had his priorities right, but the fact that the club owner had not appeared on the last day of the season to say something, anything, hurt. The assumption was that Dennis would remain, but as he put it: 'it would be nice if some fucker told me that'.

After fulfilling a promise to the Shire Supporters' Association to attend their annual awards ceremony in the Sticky Carpet, the manager without portfolio set out to roll some heads. Nine players would be asked to stay, including the Players' Player of the Year (Derek Ure) and the Fans' Player of the Year (Ure again).

The Fans' Young Player of the Year (Stephen Oates, who is actually, as a puzzled Ure pointed out, older than the Player of the Year) signed a new £10-a-week contract, as did the Coventry Branch of the Shire Supporters' Association Player of the Year (Scott Livingstone). Bucket and Spade signed on again and so did Johnny Walker, the veteran custodian Derek Jackson and Chris Miller, the full-back who played only three league games the whole season. Shaggy would begin his second successive season as the only Norwegian playing senior football in Scotland.

The old-timers – Graham McGhee and Jamie McKay – were shown the door, along with new father and recovering alcoholic, Derek Rae – although he did find employment as a fitness instructor at a Glasgow gym.

The Cat was told to come in pre-season and demonstrate to the manager that he had been working on his kicking deficiencies. Paul Ross and Grant Findlay were farmed out to junior clubs and Gordon Parks and Jamie Dunbar went back to amateur football. Greig Denham will be playing for

Stenhousemuir, the Shire's fierce derby rivals in the season 2005/6. The unkindest cut of all.

Ross Donaldson – cult hero of a thousand Airdrie pubs – was sent his jotters, along with a reminder that he had been fined two weeks' wages for missing training. Two weeks later, the original letter landed back on Les Thomson's desk, with some handwritten information from Her Majesty's Post Office scrawled across the front. 'Not known at this address,' it read.

Newall should have little difficulty in finding replacements, although the quality, and sanity, of those replacements remains questionable. In the week before the Peterhead match, the manager took a phone call in his office, relayed in the usual way by Les Thomson.

'Is that the manager?'

'Aye, I'm Dennis Newall.'

'I want to sign for you.'

'Who do you play for?'

'Well, no-one at the moment, but I can do a job for you.'

'Wait a minute, what experience have you had?'

'Enough to know I can do a job for you.'

'Look, son, I have players here who cost £100,000 in their day. I have two players with SPL experience. This is a professional, senior football side.'

'Yeah, but they haven't done much for you, have they?'

'Who?'

'Your players.'

'In terms of what?'

'Results.'

'Look, whoever you are, I think you are wasting my time and your time. If I thought you were any good I would have you scouted and maybe get you a start in a junior side. Then we can take it from there.'

'Well, you can watch me any time you want.'

'Where?'

'Up the local park.'

Perhaps the Shire's most famous former manager had it about right when he said, albeit in a slightly different context: 'Football. Bloody hell.'

THE END

Cast of Characters

Alan James Mackin, chairman. Age 49. Property developer from Paisley. Former footballer noted for his fierce commitment. The *éminence grise* of East Stirlingshire FC and, to many of the Shire support, the villain of the piece. Titular owner. Conspicuous by his absence from Firs Park for most of the season.

Leslie Grant Thomson, chief executive, secretary. Age 61. From Larbert. Former Falkirk captain and a friend of Sir Alex Ferguson. Held the purse strings at the Shire and looked after the day-to-day running of the club – with guidance from afar from the chairman.

Alexander Meikle McCabe, retired. Age 56. From Pailey. Regarded as the financial mastermind of the Shire board of directors, McCabe was often the calming voice of reason during tempestuous board meetings. Friend of the chairman.

Douglas Morrison, schoolteacher. Age 43. From Greenock. The quiet man. Another friend of Mackin's brought on to the board in controversial circumstances. With Mackin and McCabe, made up the Gang of Three who held the majority vote on the board.

Alexander Simpson Hutchison Forsyth, retired. Age 75. From Falkirk. Longest-serving director, also the oldest and feistiest. Brought on to the board as reward for services as chief scout. Also ran the Shire lottery for a time. Avid line-dancer.

John Myles Downie Morton, water jetter. Age 47. From Falkirk. Son-in-law of Alex Forsyth. The board's largest, and friendliest, character. With his elderly relative, outnumbered by the Mackin cabal, but never gave up fighting.

THE MANAGEMENT

Manager – **Dennis Newall**. Age 51. Sales executive from Glasgow. The man in the hot seat. Erudite, witty and capable, but fighting a battle against the odds in attempting to build a football team with minimal resources. Not surprisingly, blistered the paintwork at every Third Division ground in Scotland.

Assistant manager – **Greig Denham**. Age 28. Former SPL player, whose career had been savaged by injury, but was determined to plug on gamely with the Shire. Keen to get into coaching, but was stymied by club's reluctance to help in that direction. Moved on to Stenhousemuir at the end of the season.

The backroom staff – **Jimmy Wilson**, groundsman, kit manager; **Bobby Jack**, assistant kit manager; **Laura Gillogley**, physio, **David Jenkins**, physio.

THE PLAYERS

Chris Baldwin. Age 21. Midfielder. IKEA sales assistant from Edinburgh. Talented runner with pace and balance. Too easily muted by hurly-burly of the Scottish Third Division. Good diver, though. Given a free transfer at the end of the season. Nickname: Baldo.

Ross Donaldson. Age 27. Striker. Delivery driver from Bellshill. Shaven-headed, snarling cult hero of the Shire. Massive strength on the ball, but with the turning circle of the QE2. Goals tally of three considered poor return by Shire management. Won't be there for the 2005/6 season. Nickname: Roscoe.

Grant Findlay. Age 19. Striker. Student from Glasgow. Ever-present, whole-hearted trier who found first team starts limited. Farmed out to a junior club at end of season.

Ross Gilpin. Age 20. Goalkeeper. Postman from Edinburgh. Started promisingly and looked able to mount a strong challenge to be acknowledged as the number one No 1. Arrival of new goalkeeper changed all that and left in high dudgeon. Nickname: Gumbo.

David Harvey. Age 20. Full-back. Student from Bellshill. Formerly on Falkirk books. Talented defender but smitten early on by Curse of the Shire. Two own goals in one game made him top scorer for a while. Ever-present until injured late in season. Given a free transfer at the end of the season. Nickname: Harv.

Derek Jackson. Age 39. Goalkeeper. Prison officer from

Stirling. Veteran shot-stopper who spent ten seasons with Arbroath before moving to Sauchie Juniors. Moved back to the big time with East Stirling during January 2005 transfer window and staying on. Nickname: Jacko.

Scott Livingstone. Age 25. Midfielder. Surveyor from Falkirk. The Shire's most consistent, and probably the speediest, player, able to perform on both flanks. Once voted Britain's 10th Sexiest Schoolboy, but has never allowed that to go to his head. Back again for next season. Nickname: Schoolboy.

Jamie McKay. Age 23. Defender. Insurance advisor from Glasgow. Bulky (too bulky according to the management) stopper and rabid Celtic fan. One of the old guard and found himself marginalised when new management arrived. Let go at end of season.

Graham McGhee. Age 23. Defender. Cooper from Coatbridge. Another long-serving Shire player, and former captain, who found himself almost surplus to requirements when Newall and Denham swept in. Plugged away with grace and good humour, but released at end of season. Nickname: G.

Chris McGroarty. Age 24. Midfielder. Unemployed, from Airdrie. The Shire's major signing coup. A former SPL player with Dunfermline and a Scotland Under-21 cap. Made a rip-roaring start, but then seemed to be dragged down to the level of those around him. Given a free transfer at the end of the season.

Chris Miller. Age 23. Defender. Freight agent from Paisley. Luckless full-back who scored with a stunning free-kick against Gretna early on – and then was injured and spent the rest of the season on the sidelines but will be back to try his luck again next season. Nickname: Young Maurice Malpas.

Tony Mitchell. Age 25. Goalkeeper. Architect from Glasgow. The Cat. Like his namesake from England's World Cup side of 1970, had his good days and bad days. At his best a fine shot-stopper. Pre-match warm-up well worth seeing. Fate rests on improvement of goal-kicking before start of next season. Nickname: The Cat.

Stephen Oates. Age 21. Defender. Student from Falkirk. Raw-boned and very raw defender. Physically gifted but impetuous at times. Good in the air, less so on the ground. Found the going tough late on in the season. Back for next season. Nickname: Oatesy.

Gordon Parks. Age 32. Striker. Journalist from Glasgow. The life and soul of the Shire party. Found first-team starts a rarity, but regarded as the Shire supersub. Almost won the first game against Gretna. Amateur football beckons next season. Nickname: Parksy.

Derek Rae. Age 30. Midfielder. Fitness instructor from Glasgow. Reformed hell-raiser and brother of Alex of Rangers' fame. Found his chances limited – not fit enough according to the manager – but showed touches of class in rare appearances. Found alternative employment as a fitness instructor. Nickname: Del.

Joe Robertson. Age 27. Forward. Unemployed taxi driver/labourer from Clydebank. Archetypal wee Weegie with aggression and attitude. Club captain for a time but had severe problems with travelling to and from Firs Park. Left when Gordon Parks was suspended.

Paul Ross. Age 20. Midfielder. Football coach from Glasgow. Sun-tanned glamour boy (at least that's how the management regarded him) who found himself the dressing-room whipping boy. Stuck it out gamely. Moved on to a junior club.

Carl Erich Thywissen. Age 27. Midfielder. Born in Leicester but transplanted to Norway at the age of two. Tall, gangling playmaker who offered a threat in the air. Pound for pound (money that is) arguably Scotland's best foreign import, and will continue to be next season. Nickname: Shaggy.

Mark Tyrell. Age 23. Defender. Roofer from Kilsyth. Talented and occasionally cultured defender who arrived at Firs Park just after brother Paul. Signed on for 2005/6. Nickname: Spade.

Paul Tyrell. Age 24. Midfielder. Roofer from Kilsyth. The Tank. Arrived mid-season and became a massive presence in Shire midfield. Signed on for 2005/6. Nickname: Bucket.

Derek Ure. Age 20. Striker. Plumber from Falkirk. Season's top scorer (six) after a shaky start when he found it difficult to win first-team place. Pacey and athletic. Sometimes froze in front of goal. Players' Player of the Year. Back for 2005/6. Nickname: Del.

Johnny Walker. Age 31. Midfielder. Jack of all trades from Glasgow. Elevated to club captaincy and did a fine job under trying circumstances. Sweeper role seemed to suit him. Aggressive, streetwise. A winner. Remaining at Firs Park for 2005/6.

A Season in Statistics

BELLS SCOTTISH FOOTBALL LEAGUE CHAMPIONSHIP THIRD DIVISION

Date / Venue / Team / Result / Final Score / HT Score / Scorers / Attendance

Aug

Date	Venue	Team	Result	Final Score	HT Score	Scorers	Attendance
7	A	Peterhead	L	0-5	0-2		561
14	H	Gretna	L	1-2	1-2	Miller 37	276
21	A	Stenhousemuir	L	0-6	0-1		411
28	A	Cowdenbeath	L	1-2	1-0	Trialist 11*	232

Sept

Date	Venue	Team	Result	Final Score	HT Score	Scorers	Attendance
4	H	Elgin C	L	0-1	0-0		617
11	A	East Fife	L	0-1	0-1		425
18	H	Queen's Park	L	0-5	0-2		335
25	A	Albion R	D	3-3	3-3	Ure 14, Robertson 17, Thywisson 30	225

Oct

Date	Venue	Team	Result	Final Score	HT Score	Scorers	Attendance
2	H	Montrose	D	1-1	1-0	Robertson 17	247
16	A	Gretna	L	1-8	1-4	Ure 9	468
23	H	Peterhead	L	1-2	0-1	Robertson 78 (pen)	281
30	H	Cowdenbeath	L	0-2	0-1		637

Nov

Date	Venue	Team	Result	Final Score	HT Score	Scorers	Attendance
6	A	Elgin C	W	3-1	0-0	Thywisson 65, 73, Robertson 79	502
13	H	East Fife	D	1-1	1-1	Oates 34	364
27	A	Queen's Park	D	0-0	0-0		457

Trialist* (Robertson)

POINTLESS

Dec

4	H	Albion R	D	1-1	0-1	Robertson 87 (pen)	262
27	A	Peterhead	L	0-3	0-2		647

Jan

8	A	Cowdenbeath	L	2-3	2-1	Mackay 36, Robertson 44	212
15	H	Elgin C	L	0-3	0-1		191
29	H	Queen's Park	W	3-1	3-1	Trialist 4, 15**, Diack 37 (pen)	317

Feb

5	A	Albion R	D	1-1	0-0	Oates 49	350
12	H	Montrose	L	1-2	0-0	Ure 57	198
15	A	East Fife	L	0-2	0-1		441
19	A	Stenhousemuir	L	2-3	0-1	Livingstone 47, Donaldson 74	518

Mar

1	A	Montrose	L	1-4	1-1	McGroarty 11	270
5	A	Elgin C	D	0-0	0-0		394
8	H	Gretna	L	0-4	0-2		185
12	H	Cowdenbeath	W	2-1	0-1	McGroarty 48, P. Tyrrell 60	204
15	H	Stenhousemuir	W	3-2	2-0	Donaldson 3, McGroarty 20, Ross 68	211
19	H	East Fife	W	1-0	1-0	Ure 24	315

Apr

2	A	Queen's Park	L	0-2	0-1		486
9	A	Montrose	L	1-4	1-1	Ure 22	329
16	H	Albion R	L	0-2	0-1		204
23	H	Stenhousemuir	L	1-4	1-3	Oates 43	242
30	A	Gretna	L	0-1	0-1		1,585

May

7	H	Peterhead	L	1-5	0-3	Ure 82	192

Trialist** (McGroarty)

Final table

	P	W	D	L	F	A	W	D	L	F	A	GD	Pts
			Home					Away					
Gretna	36	18	0	0	70	10	14	2	2	60	19	101	98
Peterhead	36	11	6	1	46	17	12	3	3	35	21	43	78
Cowdenbeath	36	8	4	6	24	32	6	5	7	30	29	-7	51
Queen's Park	36	7	5	6	24	24	6	4	8	27	26	1	48
Montrose	36	7	2	9	27	29	6	5	7	20	24	-6	46
Elgin C	36	7	5	6	24	31	5	2	11	15	30	-22	43
Stenhousemuir	36	5	7	6	31	25	5	5	8	27	33	0	42
East Fife	36	7	4	7	17	19	3	4	11	23	37	-16	38
Albion R	36	3	4	11	20	46	5	6	7	20	32	-38	34
East Stirling	36	4	3	11	17	39	1	4	13	15	49	-56	22

BELL'S CHALLENGE CUP

First Round

July

31	H	Berwick R		L	1-2	0-1	Donaldson 59	264

CIS INSURANCE CUP

First Round

Aug

10	H	Peterhead		L	2-3	1-1	Ure 60, Parks 84	482

STIRLINGSHIRE CUP

Aug

17	H	Dumbarton		L	0-3	0-0		162

Sept

7	A	Falkirk		L	0-5	0-2		1,377

POINTLESS

TENNENT'S CUP

First Round

Nov

23   A   Morton   L 1-3   1-3   Livingstone 9   1,902